Rose Petals

A Devotional

Rose Reggiacorte Sieber

OlivePress
צהר זית

Messianic & Christian Publisher

Rose Petals

A DEVOTIONAL

Rose Reggiacorte Sieber

OlivePress
צהר זית
Publisher

Rose Petals A Devotional

ISBN: 978-1-941173-17-6

Published by

Olive Press Messianic and Christian Publisher
olivepresspublisher.com

Printed in the USA

Cover and interior design by Olive Press

All rose photos © 2016 by Hans Seiber, the author's husband

In honor to God, all pronouns referring to the Trinity are capitalized; satan's names are not.

All Scriptures unless otherwise noted are taken from *The King James Version*, public domain, with most ancient words like "thee" and "thou" and ancient verb endings like on "cometh" updated by the author .

One Scripture (on the opposite page) marked NIV is taken from the *Holy Bible, New International Version.* Copyright © 1973, 1978, 1984 by International Bible Society. All rights reserved.

One Scripture (on p. 177) marked NASB is taken from the NEW AMERICAN STANDARD BIBLE®. Copyright © 1960, 1962, 1963, 1968, 1971, 1972, 1973, 1975, 1977, 1995 by The Lockman Foundation. Used by permission.

One Scripture (on p. 15) marked NRSV is taken from the New Revised Standard Version of the Bible, copyright © 1989 National Council of the Churches of Christ in the USA. Used by permission. All rights reserved.

I am the rose of Sharon...

Song of Songs 2:1

Ointment and perfume rejoice the heart.

Proverbs 27:9

For we are to God the pleasing aroma of Christ....

II Corinthians 2:15 NIV

Table of Contents

Dear Reader   8

January   9

February   32

March   50

April   71

May   89

June   111

July   125

August   141

September   158

October   176

November   193

December   210

Dear Reader,

This little book came to pass because everyday I need words of affirmation, comfort and wisdom from God. As I listen, He speaks the encouragement I need and cannot find anywhere else. Eventually, I felt to compile some of these simple words into this book. Hopefully, it motivates you to also look and listen to Him and the Bible. I pray this book leads you to enjoy relating and conversing with Him, if you do not do so already. He will enrich your life more than anything else can.

Lovingly, Rose

Here's what I sensed from the Lord about this book:

"My purpose for your writing is not to make you known or show clever words and wit. It's simply to encourage others to recognize My truth in response to the everyday needs of My people. I hear and see your life situations and I respond as a loving Father."

January

January 1

"For the eyes of the Lord run to and fro throughout the whole earth, to show Himself strong in the behalf of them whose heart is perfect toward Him." II Chronicles 16:9

"O taste and see that the Lord is good: blessed is the man that trusts in Him." Psalm 34:8

"Like as a father pities his children, so the Lord pities him that fear Him." Psalm 103:13

"And this is love, that we walk after His commandments." II John 6

"Look across the years with My eyes and heart. Glean the wisdom, but leave and forget the daily cost. Gather the gold, the close companionship of mind and heart and distribute it with great joy, laughter and abundance. Let others taste and see how good and real I am. I am the dear, understanding Father all desire to have: the closest Friend possible who makes life a journey of purpose with a glorious ending. Be and live and give as children of the King, the Creator of the universe."

January 2

"Serve the Lord with gladness: come before His presence with singing."
Psalm 100:2

Jesus said, "I am the vine, you are the branches: He that abides in Me, and I in him, the same brings forth much fruit: for without Me you can do nothing." John 15:5

"Whatsoever your hand finds to do, do it with your might; for there is no work, nor device, nor knowledge, nor wisdom in the grave, where you go." Ecclesiastes 9:10

"And whatsoever we ask, we receive of Him, because we keep His commandments, and do those things that are pleasing in His sight." 1 John 3:22

"Be kind and interested in all. Take time for the other. Bring forth fruit and distribute it widely. Daily, take notice that all before you are in need of Me. Cheer and serve without reserve those around you; a prayer, a smile, a good word, a helping hand. Notice every opportunity I bring to enrich another, and thereby making life joyful, fruitful and pleasing to Me."

January 3

"He makes the storm a calm, so that the waves thereof are still." Psalm 107:29

"Behold, the days come, says the Lord, that I will raise unto David a righteous Branch, and a King shall reign and prosper, and shall execute judgment and justice in the earth." Jeremiah 23:5

"And they sing the song of Moses the servant of God, and the song of the Lamb, saying, Great and marvelous are Your works, Lord God Almighty; just and true are Your ways, You King of saints." Revelation 15:3

"Jesus said unto him, Thomas, because you have seen Me, you have believed: blessed are they that have not seen, and yet have believed." John 20:29

"Calm yourself about the injustices of this world. Remember, I am perfect justice. Eventually, I right all the wrongs in ways you cannot imagine, down to the smallest details. Much tragedy could be avoided if man would believe Me and obey Me."

January 4

"And I saw the dead, small and great, stand before God; and the books were opened: and another book was opened, which is the book of life: and the dead were judged out of those things which were written in the books, according to their works." Revelation 20:12

"He that has the Son has life; and he that has not the Son of God has not life." 1 John 5:12

"Choosing rather to suffer affliction with the people of God, than to enjoy the pleasures of sin for a season." Hebrews 11:25

"For what shall it profit a man, if he shall gain the whole world, and lose his own soul?" Mark 8:36

"Yes, your life is a story, an adventure, whereby Christ is formed in you by My individual training, if you will surrender and co-operate and co-labor with My Spirit. Thereby are you made rich and truly alive. The choice is yours alone. Every man must choose Me alone, and learn to be content with Me alone. Thereby is true gain and successful living."

January 5

Jesus said, "It is impossible but that offences will come: but woe unto him, through whom they come! Luke 17:1

"Follow peace with all men, and holiness, without which no man shall see the Lord: Looking diligently lest any man fail the grace of God; lest any root of bitterness springing up trouble you, and thereby many be defiled." Hebrews 12:14-15

"For the weapons of our warfare are not carnal, but mighty through God to the pulling down of strongholds; Casting down imaginations, and every high thing that exalts itself against the knowledge of God, and bringing into captivity every thought to the obedience of Christ." II Corinthians 10:4-5

"Even a fool, when he holds his peace, is counted wise: and he that shuts his lips is esteemed a man of understanding." Proverbs 17:28

"Take no offence, hold no bitterness against those who are lost in the ways of the world. They do not know what they are about. Don't fall prey to vain imaginations and deceptive thinking. You are set apart for Me, and these matters are not your concern, but are mine. It pleases Me when you hold your peace."

January 6

"If we say that we have fellowship with Him, and walk in darkness, we lie, and do not the truth." 1 John 1:6

"But if we walk in the light, as He is in the light, we have fellowship one with another, and the blood of Jesus Christ His Son cleanses us from all sin. If we say that we have no sin, we deceive ourselves, and the truth is not in us." 1 John 1:7-8

Jesus said, "...the devil ... he was a murderer from the beginning, and abode not in the truth because there is no truth in him." John 8:44

Jesus said, "I thank you, o Father, Lord of Heaven and earth, because You have hid these things from the wise and prudent, and have revealed them unto babes." Matthew 11:25

"You learn to walk in the light by allowing Me to bring everything into My light. Your enemy would want to keep you in darkness. I am a God of true revelation to your heart. When you say yes to Me, you must continue to say, daily, yes to My necessary revelation. It's My very nature to expose lies by My great, bright truth that no man can change or avoid."

January 7

Jesus said, "And you yourselves like unto men that wait for their Lord, when He will return from the wedding; that when He comes and knocks, they may open unto Him immediately." Luke 12:36

"Wait on the Lord: be of good courage, and He shall strengthen thine heart: wait, I say, on the Lord." Psalm 27:14

"Hear me, O Lord; for Your loving kindness is good: turn unto me according to the multitude of Your tender mercies." Psalm 69:16

"The Lord of hosts hath sworn, saying, Surely as I have thought, so shall it come to pass; and as I have purposed, so shall it stand." Isaiah 14:24

"Wait upon Me. A waiter is one ready and instant to serve. Trust Me to answer your prayers as I see most profitable—in My time. My purposes are so much vaster than yours. Waiting in patience shows your trust in Me and My perfect goodness."

January 8

Jesus said, "I am Alpha and Omega, the first and the last." Revelation 1:11

"Whoso offers praise glorifies Me: and to him that orders his conversation aright will I show the salvation of God." Psalm 50:23

Jesus said, "If a man love Me, he will keep My Words: and My Father will love him, and We will come unto him, and make Our abode with him." John 14:23

"Give heed to My reproof; I will pour out My thoughts to you; I will make My Words known to you." Proverbs 1:23 (NRSV)

"Then Samuel answered, Speak; for your servant hears." 1 Samuel 3:10

"A living relationship with Me means a continuous relationship with Me. Think on Me first and converse with Me as you plan your day. Let Me show you what is in My mind and heart. See that My ideas and words confirm the best for you and others."

January 9

Jesus said, "I am the living bread which came down from Heaven: if any man eat of this bread, he shall live forever: and the bread that I will give is My flesh, which I will give for the life of the world." John 6:51

"Now unto Him that is able to do exceeding abundantly above all that we ask or think, according to the power that works in us, Unto Him be glory in the church by Christ Jesus throughout all ages, world without end. Amen." Ephesians 3:20-21

"For Godly sorrow works repentance to salvation not to be repented of: but the sorrow of the world works death." 11 Corinthians 7:10

Jesus said, "If therefore you have not been faithful in the unrighteous mammon, who will commit to your trust the true riches?" Luke 16:11

I have provided for your every need. Looking to My Son for the gift of repentance and My forgiveness, is the gift that gives you My peace. Walking through your life, holding My hand makes all My rich gifts available to you. The true riches are only available to My children."

January 10

Jesus said, "My grace is sufficient for you: for My strength is made perfect in weakness." II Corinthians 12:9

Jesus said, "Be you therefore perfect, even as your Father which is in Heaven is perfect." Matthew 5:48

"My flesh and my heart fail: but God is the strength of my heart, and my portion forever." Psalm 73:26

"But you, O Lord, are a God full of compassion, and gracious, longsuffering, and plenteous in mercy and truth." Psalm 86:15

"My grace is sufficient for all the needs and suffering of your life. In all I do, there is perfect balance. You discover this by experiencing life with Me, learning of Me. In your natural life, you will miss the balance, you will have failures. Take heart, I am gracious. Be ever learning how to maintain right balance as you grow in Me."

January 11

"But I keep under my body, and bring it into subjection: lest that by any means, when I have preached to others, I myself should be a castaway." 1 Corinthians 9:27

"Rise up, you women that are at ease; hear My voice, you careless daughters; give ear unto My speech." Isaiah 32:9

"Blessed is the man that endures temptation: for when he is tried, he shall receive the crown of life, which the Lord has promised to them that love Him." James 1:12

Jesus said, "If any man will come after Me, let him deny himself, and take up his cross daily, and follow Me." Luke 9:23

"Yes, keep under your flesh. What others might do, you cannot. Temptations would call you to take your ease and enjoy the pleasures that abound for body and soul. But you are My disciple. My plan for your life requires a corrected course of self denial. You need to feel at peace and favor with Me and with yourself. So, come away from other voices and hear Mine first."

January 12

"Then He called His twelve disciples together, and gave them power and authority over all devils, and to cure diseases." Luke 9:1

"And be not conformed to this world: but be you transformed by the renewing of your mind, that you may prove what is that good, and acceptable, and perfect, will of God." Romans 12:2

"...when He shall appear, we shall be like Him...." 1 John 3:2

"For the Lord takes pleasure in His people: He will beautify the meek with salvation." Psalm 149:4

"Those who walk with Me for many years have an patina of dignity, grace, and authority for which many desire. This is the true beauty that endures. Continue to allow Me to transform you by renewing your thoughts in My truth. Allow the inner to create the outer qualities only I can give."

January 13

Jesus said, "I say unto you, that likewise joy shall be in Heaven over one sinner that repents, more than over ninety and nine just persons, which need no repentance." Luke 15:7

"Pride goes before destruction, and an haughty spirit before a fall." Proverbs 16:18

Jesus said, "Should not you also have had compassion on your fellow servant, even as I had pity on you?" Matthew 18:33

"For if we would judge ourselves, we should not be judged." 1 Corinthians 11:31

"Repentance is a continually needed gift. Use it liberally. It repels pride, self sufficiency, and arrogance. It keeps you dependant on Me and My leading Spirit. It keeps you in the right place to serve others with tender humility and compassion. All My gifts bring you deep righteousness, peace and joy in My Spirit's presence. You no longer can judge any man's weaknesses and failures."

January 14

Jesus said, "Behold, I stand at the door, and knock: if any man hear My voice, and open the door, I will come in to him, and will sup with him, and he with Me." Revelation 3:20

Jesus said, "No man can come to Me, except the Father which has sent Me draw him: and I will raise him up at the last day." John 6:44

"Jesus said unto them, Come and dine." John 21:12

Jesus said, "This is My commandment, That you love one another, as I have loved you. Greater love has no man than this, that a man lay down his life for his friends." John 15:12-13

"Behold, I stand at the door, and knock. I am ever inviting and looking to be invited. I exist in relationship and you must be in right relationships to be fully human and alive. My Word draws you into relationship with Me, but you must desire and welcome and enjoy this experience. I am the creator of hospitality."

January 15

"Jesus Christ the same yesterday, and today, and forever." Hebrews 13:8

"He restores my soul: He leads me in the paths of righteousness for His Name's sake." Psalm 23:3

"I will love You, O Lord, my strength." Psalm 18:1

"And call upon Me in the day of trouble: I will deliver you, and you shall glorify Me." Psalm 50:15

"I am the great replenisher. I drain away the fatigue of yesterday, and restore the joy strength for today. Stay in close communication with Me. Call upon Me, Jesus, in all situations. Acknowledge your need."

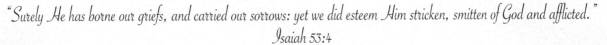

January 16

"Hereby perceive we the love of God, because He laid down His life for us: and we ought to lay down our lives for the brethren." 1 John 3:16

"Surely He has borne our griefs, and carried our sorrows: yet we did esteem Him stricken, smitten of God and afflicted." Isaiah 53:4

Jesus said, "Take heed that you despise not one of these little ones; for I say unto you, that in Heaven their angels do always behold the face of My Father which is in Heaven." Matthew 18:10

"Before I formed you in the belly I knew you; and before you came forth out of the womb I sanctified you." Jeremiah 1:5

"Most cannot grasp the great value and importance of their life. Every human life has value, purpose, and place. Life is a wonderful gift from Me. There is much sorrow on earth and in Heaven because life is not understood and treasured. Care for one another in the smallest acts, words, and prayers. I am in the little things of life."

January 17

Jesus said, "You shall love the Lord your God with all your heart, and with all your soul, and with all your mind. This is the first and great commandment. And the second is like unto it, You shall love your neighbor as yourself. On these two commandments hang all the law and prophets." Matthew 22:37-40

"If you fulfill the royal law according to the Scripture, You shall love your neighbor as yourself, you do well." James 2:8

Jesus said, "Be you therefore merciful, as your Father also is merciful. Judge not, and you shall not be judged: condemn not, and you shall not be condemned: forgive and you shall be forgiven." Luke 6:36-37

"…in lowliness of mind let each esteem others better than themselves." Philippians 2:3

"And walk in love, as Christ also has loved us, and has given Himself for us…." Ephesians 5:2

"I say, do unto others as you would have them do unto you (Matthew 7:12), because, in time, all your actions and thoughts will return to you as you have given them to others. My laws change for no man. Obey My greatest commandment of loving Me and loving others as I have loved you by laying aside self and putting others first."

January 18

"Give instruction to a wise man, and he will be yet wiser: teach a just man, and he will increase in learning." Proverbs 9:9

"How much better is it to get wisdom than gold! and to get understanding rather to be chosen than silver! Proverbs 16:16

"Whoso is wise, and will observe these things, even they shall understand the lovingkindness of the Lord." Psalm 107:43

"Blessed is the man whom You choose, and cause to approach unto You, that he may dwell in Your courts: we shall be satisfied with the goodness of Your house, even of Your holy temple." Psalm 65:4

"Learn of Me, in and from the sufferings of life on earth. Make use, good use, of your inevitable pain. Apply My truth to your experience, and gain wisdom and My perspective on what you observe. I reveal Myself to the willing, trusting, and obedient. This is enough to satisfy every desire."

January 19

Jesus said, "For everyone that asks receives; and he that seeks finds; and to him that knocks it shall be opened."
Matthew 7:8

"He will fulfill the desire of them that fear Him: He also will hear their cry, and will save them." Psalm 145:19

"For the Lord God is a sun and shield: the Lord will give grace and glory: no good thing will He withhold from them that walk uprightly." Psalm 84:11

Jesus said, "That all men should honour the Son, even as they honour the Father. He that honours not the Son honours not the Father which has sent Him." John 5:23

"You find Me, you hear Me, when you seek for Me with your whole heart, listening, waiting for Me to reveal Myself. It gives Me joy to transform your life by this relating. I do not withhold anything good and necessary from My children. But the children must recognize, honour, and obey their Father from whom they have originated."

January 20

Jesus said, "His lord said unto him, Well done, you good and faithful servant: you have been faithful over a few things, I will make you ruler over many things: enter you into the joy of your Lord." Matthew 25:21

"But let it be the hidden man of the heart, in that which is not corruptible, even the ornament of a meek and quiet spirit, which is in the sight of God of great price." 1 Peter 3:4

Jesus said, "Remember the Word that I said unto you, The servant is not greater than his Lord. If they have persecuted me, they will also persecute you; if they have kept My saying, they will keep yours also." John 15:20

Jesus said, "For whosoever will save his life shall lose it: but whosoever will lose his life for My sake, the same shall save it." Luke 9:24

"Be faithful in the everyday, mundane service to Me and others. Most of My closest friends and servants are hidden and unnoticed. Many of the most rewarded are unknown to the world. They, early on, came to know My Word is true, and decided to turn from the way of the world. My way is indeed narrow, and many who choose it suffer misunderstanding and loss. In My Kingdom this loss is gain. The choice is left to whosoever will."

January 21

"Come now, and let us reason together, says the Lord: though your sins be as scarlet, they shall be as white as snow; though they be red like crimson, they shall be as wool." Isaiah 1:18

Jesus said, "Wherefore I say unto you, her sins, which are many, are forgiven; for she loved much: but to whom little is forgiven, the same loves little." Luke 7:47

Jesus said, "And forgive us our sins; for we also forgive everyone that is indebted to us. And lead us not into temptation; but deliver us from evil." Luke 11:4

"And be you kind one to another, tenderhearted, forgiving one another, even as God for Christ's sake has forgiven you." Ephesians 4:32

"See the snow I created, and recall I have washed away your sin and made you whiter than snow. Be as forgiving of others, even if they do not know or receive your forgiveness. Those who are forgiven much, love Me greatest, and grow in capacity to forgive others."

January 22

Jesus said, "For where two or three are gathered together in My Name, there am I in the midst of them." *Matthew 18:20*

"Christ also loved the church, and gave Himself for it; That He might sanctify and cleanse it with the washing of water by the Word, That He might present it to Himself a glorious church, not having spot, or wrinkle, or any such thing; but that it should be holy and without blemish." *Ephesians 5:25-27*

"Let us be glad and rejoice, and give honour to Him: for the marriage of the Lamb is come, and His wife has made herself ready." *Revelation 19:7*

"Know you not that they which run in a race run all, but one receives the prize? So run, that you may obtain." *1 Corinthians 9:24*

"When My people gather together, I am there with them, preparing My bride. I am cleansing them with My Words of life, assisting them with their garments of praise. Be about preparing for the marriage feast. I am the God of celebration and restoration. Look up to Me, keep your eyes on the prize to come."

January 23

Jesus said, "He also that received seed among the thorns is he that hears the Word: and the care of this world, and the deceitfulness of riches, choke the Word, and he becomes unfruitful." *Matthew 13:22*

Jesus said, "It is not for you to know the times or the seasons, which the Father has put in His own power." *Acts 1:7*

"Offer the sacrifices of righteousness, and put your trust in the Lord." *Psalms 4:5*

"Commit your works unto the Lord, and your thoughts shall be established." *Proverbs 16:3*

"Dear child, put aside grey thoughts: concerns, and possibilities about the future. No one can or should know, or be concerned about the future I already know. Trust Me, your all knowing, all caring Father. Concentrate on Me today: My voice, My Word, My leading, My purposes, My character. This is sufficient for your mortal life and lifts you into My eternal life. Worship Me by your everyday labor."

January 24

"Jesus Christ the same yesterday, and to day, and forever." Hebrews 13:8

"For our light affliction, which is but for a moment, works for us a far more exceeding and eternal weight of glory; While we look not at the things which are seen, but at the things which are not seen: for the things which are seen are temporal; but the things which are not seen are eternal." II Corinthians 4:17-18

Jesus said, "If I have told you earthly things, and you believe not, how shall you believe, if I tell you of heavenly things?" John 3:12

Jesus said, "Take heed, and beware of covetousness: for a man's life consisteth not in the abundance of the things which he possesses." Luke 12:15

"I am ever the same, yet I manifest in continuous change, growth, and movement. What your natural eyes see may appear as enduring, but this is all temporal. It is My unseen world of spirit that is eternal. Those who recognize this have My freedom and can walk lightly without grasping the things of the world. I desire balance in your life. Walk with Me."

January 25

Jesus said, "In My Father's house are many mansions: if it were not so, I would have told you. I go to prepare a place for you. And if I go and prepare a place for you, I will come again, and receive you unto Myself; that where I am, there you may be also." John 14:2-3

"The grace of the Lord Jesus Christ, and the love of God, and the communion of the Holy Ghost, be with you all. Amen." II Corinthians 13:14

Jesus said, "Therefore whosoever hears these sayings of Mine, and does them, I will liken him unto a wise man, which built his house upon a rock: And the rain descended, and the floods came, and the winds blew, and beat upon that house; and it fell not: for it was founded upon a rock." Matthew 7:24-25

"The Lord takes pleasure in them that fear Him, in those that hope in His mercy." Psalm 147:11

"Yes, I am now preparing a place for you. Not only for eternity, but for now. As you commune with Me today and every day, joining your heart and thoughts with Mine, a place with Me is established. Your primary dependency is then built on Me and My power. There's no need to beg, My child. Lift all to Me in faith. My joy is to feel you close and waiting trustfully."

January 26

"Wait on the Lord, and keep His way, and He shall exalt you to inherit the land: when the wicked are cut off, you shall see it." Psalm 37:34

"Fret not yourself because of evil men, neither be you envious at the wicked." Proverbs 24:19

"And the apostles said unto the Lord, Increase our faith." Luke 17:5

"The earth is the Lord's, and the fullness thereof; the world, and they that dwell therein." Psalm 24:1

"Waiting upon Me need not be tedious or dull. I fill you with hope, My hope, that works towards good outcomes. Fret not about the turmoil and conditions in the world. Concentrate on what I say and on My leading for your sphere of influence today. You are not accountable for the choices of others. The earth and its fullness are Mine."

January 27

"Can a woman forget her sucking child, that she should not have compassion on the son of her womb? Yes, they may forget, yet will I not forget you." Isaiah 49:15

"Brethren, I count not myself to have apprehended: but this one thing I do, forgetting those things which are behind, and reaching forth unto those things which are before, I press toward the mark for the prize of the high calling of God in Christ Jesus." Philippians 3:13-14

"For His anger endures but a moment; in His favour is life: weeping may endure for a night, but joy comes in the morning." Psalm 30:5

"A new heart also will I give you, and a new spirit will I put within you: and I will take away the stony heart out of your flesh, and I will give you a heart of flesh." Ezekiel 36:26

"I never forget you. I forget your past, confessed sins. It's always a new morning in My Kingdom. Forget your regrets and condemnations and hurts to self and others. What is forgiven must be left behind. Reckon on the new, fresh beginning I give you each day. This is a precious gift to all My children: My smile upon you."

January 28

"Every good gift and every perfect gift is from above, and comes down from the Father of lights, with whom is no variableness, neither shadow of turning." James 1:17

Jesus said, "Verily, verily, I say unto you, Moses gave you not that bread from Heaven; but My Father gives you the true bread from Heaven." John 6:32

"Oh that men would praise the Lord for His goodness, and for His wonderful works to the children of men!" Psalm 107:8

"Let not your heart envy sinners: but be you in the fear of the Lord all the day long." Proverbs 23:17

"Yes, every good gift comes from Me. This knowledge will cheer you anytime you remember My goodness with a thankful heart. Be of good cheer. Envy not the situations of the Godless and lost ones."

January 29

"Because you have made the Lord, which is my refuge, even the Most High, your habitation; There shall no evil befall you, neither shall any plague come nigh your dwelling." Psalm 91:9-10

"Be strong and of a good courage, fear not, nor be afraid of them: for the Lord your God, He it is that does go with you; He will not fail you, nor forsake you." Deuteronomy 31:6

"But the day of the Lord will come as a thief in the night; in the which the heavens shall pass away with a great noise, and the elements shall melt with fervent heat, the earth also and the works that are therein shall be burned up." II Peter 3:10

"You are of God, little children, and have overcome them: because greater is He that is in you, than he that is in the world." 1 John 4:4

"Have I not proven to you My protection and care through many years of danger and need? You dwell in My secret place, under My care. I speak to My children of things to come, so they are not surprised by sudden calamity. Be courageous and resourceful, as I prepare you to live and rescue many in the darkest time ahead."

January 30

Jesus said, "Enter you in at the strait gate: for wide is the gate, and broad is the way, that leads to destruction, and many there be which go in thereat: Because strait is the gate, and narrow is the way, which leads unto life, and few there be that find it." Matthew 7:13-14

"But of the times and the seasons, brethren, you have no need that I write unto you. For yourselves know perfectly that the day of the Lord so comes as a thief in the night." 1 Thessalonians 5:1-2

"Set your affection on things above, not on things of the earth. For you are dead, and your life is hid with Christ in God." Colossians 3:2-3

"For the Lord will not cast off His people, neither will He forsake His inheritance." Psalm 94:14

"Fear not the days of destruction coming. My power and plan are far greater than any plan of mankind, or the enemy. Fear not what any man can do to you. Your true life and destiny are hidden in Me. Even your concern to leave a legacy is not a matter of great importance."

January 31

Jesus said, *"And when they bring you unto the synagogues, and unto magistrates, and powers, take you no thought how or what thing you shall answer, or what you shall say: For the Holy Ghost shall teach you in the same hour what you ought to say."* Luke 12:11-12

"Your shoes shall be iron and brass; and as your days, so shall your strength be." Deuteronomy 33:25

"Then He answered and spoke unto me, saying, This is the Word of the Lord unto Zerubbabel, saying, Not by might, nor by power, but by My Spirit, says the Lord of hosts." Zechariah 4:6

"Serve the Lord with gladness: come before His presence with singing." Psalm 100:2

"Take no thought for tomorrow. I am already in all your tomorrows. According to your days, is My strength sufficient. Trouble yourself not with doubts concerning your ability to meet challenges ahead. It is not going to be by what you can manage to do, but by your surrender to what My Spirit is doing and wants to do. Follow Me and serve Me with gladness, moment by glorious moment."

February

February 1

"Charity suffers long, and is kind; charity envies not; charity vaunts not itself, is not puffed up." 1 Corinthians 13:4

"If we suffer, we shall also reign with Him: if we deny Him, He also will deny us." II Timothy 2:12

"For this is good and acceptable in the sight of God our Saviour; Who will have all men to be saved, and to come unto the knowledge of the truth." 1 Timothy 2:3-4

"Let this mind be in you, which was also in Christ Jesus." Philippians 2:5

"Everything has a purpose, even suffering and pain. Many suffer for the sins and ignorance of others. No one is beyond the influence and consequences of others' choices, good or bad. Much is created by collective thought, agreed upon beliefs. My desire is for all to come to know and believe Me. To join Me in this most noble work is of highest importance. Evaluate not by what you see, but by My mind which you can know by My Spirit."

February 2

"But though our outward man perish, yet the inward man is renewed day by day." II Corinthians 4:16

"O house of Jacob, come you, and let us walk in the light of the Lord." Isaiah 2:5

"And you are complete in Him, which is the head of all principality and power." Colossians 2:10

"The blessing of the Lord, it makes rich, and He adds no sorrow with it." Proverbs 10:22

Yes, your outer person wears down, but your inner life is built up more rich and deep as the years of your life on earth continue. Discovering and experiencing this gives your life a completeness and perspective available only to My children who walk in My light. Gone is the regret, confusion, and sorrow. All is clear in My law of sowing and reaping."

February 3

Jesus said, "Behold, I stand at the door, and knock: if any man hear My voice, and open the door, I will come in to him, and will sup with him, and he with Me." Revelation 3:20

Jesus said, "Likewise, I say unto you, there is joy in the presence of the angels of God over one sinner that repents." Luke 15:10

"... but David encouraged himself in the Lord his God." 1 Samuel 30:6

"But Moses' hands were heavy; and they took a stone, and put it under him, and he sat thereon; and Aaron and Hur stayed up his hands, the one on the one side, and the other on the other side; and his hands were steady until the going down of the sun." Exodus 17:12

"Behold, I stand at the door and knock. It's a glorious day when one hears and opens to Me. Think on this, and remember; survey what I have transformed in you and those around you. Encourage yourself in that you are Mine, and available to those seeking Me. Holding up the arms of those leading My cause is a noble, worthwhile calling. Answer and be glad."

February 4

"Trust in the Lord with all your heart; and lean not unto your own understanding. In all your ways acknowledge Him, and He shall direct your paths. Be not wise in your own eyes: fear the Lord, and depart from evil." Proverbs 3:5-7

"The king's heart is in the hand of the Lord, as the rivers of water: He turns it whithersoever He will." Proverbs 21:1

"I love them that love Me; and those that seek Me early shall find Me." Proverbs 8:17

"The steps of a good man are ordered by the Lord: and he delights in His way." Psalm 37:23

"To not lean on your own understanding requires trust in Me and My way. Observe My hand at work, and receive wisdom. Seek Me early, and depend upon Me to direct your thoughts and steps."

February 5

"All my springs are in You." Psalm 87:7

"Let the words of my mouth, and the meditation of my heart, be acceptable in Your sight, O Lord, my strength, and my redeemer." Psalm 19:14

Jesus said, "If any man thirst, let him come unto Me, and drink." John 7:37

"And now abides faith, hope, charity, these three; but the greatest of these is charity." 1 Corinthians 13:13

"Hope springs from ever renewing faith in Me, and fellowship with Me, everyday. I am renewing your mind as you meditate on My words. Old words and new words that are ever flowing. My living waters will never cease. It is you that must continually drink to replenish your faith, hope, and abundant charity."

February 6

"*Therefore say unto the house of Israel, Thus says the Lord God; Repent, and turn yourselves from your idols; and turn away your faces from all your abominations.*" *Ezekiel 14:6*

"*But as it is written, Eye has not seen, nor ear heard, neither have entered into the heart of man, the things which God has prepared for them that love Him.*" *1 Corinthians 2:9*

"*Whereas you know not what shall be on the morrow. For what is your life? It is even a vapor, that appears for a little time, and then vanishes away.*" *James 4:14*

"*Love not the world, neither the things that are in the world. If any man love the world, the love of the Father is not in him. For all that is in the world, the lust of the flesh, and the lust of the eyes, and the pride of life, is not of the Father, but is of the world. And the world passes away, and the lust thereof: but he that does the will of God abides forever.*"
1 John 2:15-17

"Keep yourself from idols. Worship nothing of the world. Enjoy My manifold gifts as a visitor, honored and cared for. Remember the brevity of life on earth, and the place of growth and learning that it is. Keep yourself from the deceptions of man. I bring all things to their rightful conclusion. Only those who know Me can experience eternity."

February 7

"…endure hardness, as a good soldier of Jesus Christ." II Timothy 2:3

"Finally, my brethren, be strong in the Lord, and in the power of His might." Ephesians 6:10

"Be not overcome of evil, but overcome evil with good." Romans 12:21

"O the depth of the riches both of the wisdom and knowledge of God! How unsearchable are His judgments, and His ways past finding out!" Romans 11:33

"Endure hardness as a good soldier. These are days where you must be strong and of good courage to recognize the true condition of the world, and not despair. Know that I have a large and good plan for My people, and the good will overcome the evil. Still, I say rejoice and be glad in your small part of My great dream for mankind."

February 8

"And it shall come to pass in the last days, says God, I will pour out of My Spirit upon all flesh: and your sons and your daughters shall prophesy, and your young men shall see visions, and your old men shall dream dreams." Acts 2:17

"That the God of our Lord Jesus Christ, the Father of glory, may give unto you the Spirit of wisdom and revelation in the knowledge of Him." Ephesians 1:17

"Watch therefore, for you know neither the day not the hour wherein the Son of Man comes." Matthew 25:13

"Be you also patient; stablish your hearts: for the coming of the Lord draws nigh." James 5:8

"These are the days of My pouring out of My Spirit on all the earth. My people see clearly, and can prophesy My works with understanding. Be strong. Be patient. Be watching, for I am indeed returning to earth for My own."

February 9

Jesus said, "And I will pray the Father, and He shall give you another Comforter, that He may abide with you forever." John 14:16

"The Lord is good, a stronghold in the day of trouble; and He knows them that trust in Him." Nahum 1:7

"Trust in Him at all times; you people, pour out your heart before Him: God is a refuge for us." Psalm 62:8

"Now our Lord Jesus Christ Himself, and God, even our Father, which has loved us, and has given us everlasting consolation and good hope through grace, Comfort your hearts, and stablish you in every good word and work." 11 Thessalonians 2:16-17

"My comfort is real, true and available to whosoever will. In whatever loss or need, My refuge is secure. I foresaw all when I left My Spirit with you. For those whose hearts live in Me, I am an ever present consolation. My Spirit is a great gift from a protective, deeply loving Father."

February 10

"But grow in grace, and in the knowledge of our Lord and Saviour Jesus Christ. To Him be glory both now and forever. Amen." II Peter 3:18

"Withhold not good from them to whom it is due, when it is in the power of your hand to do it." Proverbs 3:27

Jesus said, "Every branch in Me that bears not fruit He takes away: and every branch that bears fruit, He purges it, that it may bring forth more fruit." John 15:2

"Again, I considered all travail, and every right work, that for this a man is envied of his neighbor. This is also vanity and vexation of spirit." Ecclesiastes 4:4

"Grow in grace. Give everyone what they need, but don't always deserve. This is only possible by My gracious Spirit and true words. Stay in simplicity, and freedom from longing for what others may have. Trust in My sufficiency, wise pruning, delays, and holding back what is not good for you today."

"*Horror has taken hold upon me because of the wicked that forsake Your law.*" Psalm 119:53

Jesus said, "O faithless and perverse generation, how long shall I be with you, and suffer you?" Luke 9:41

*Jesus said, "For God sent not His Son into the world to condemn the world;
but that the world through Him might be saved.*" John 3:17

"*He is despised and rejected of men; a man of sorrows and acquainted with grief: and we hid as it were our faces from
Him; He was despised, and we esteemed Him not.*" Isaiah 53:3

"You see and feel for man's debasement and horrifying events due to his blind choices on earth. Think,
I have seen it for centuries, eons. Therefore, I sent My Son to show men the way out of their dark
thoughts and sinful ways. You share My grief that men refuse My gift and hope."

February 12

*Paul said, "Unto me, who am less than the least of all saints, is this grace given, that I
should preach among the Gentiles the unsearchable riches of Christ.*" Ephesians 3:8

"*I have seen his ways, and will heal him: I will lead him also, and restore comforts unto him and to his mourners.*"
Isaiah 57:18

"*Receive My instruction, and not silver; and knowledge rather than choice gold. For wisdom is better than rubies; and all
the things that may be desired are not to be compared to it.* Proverbs 8:10-11

*Jesus said, "Go home to your friends, and tell them how great things the Lord has done for you,
and has had compassion on you.*" Mark 5:19

"I have made you rich and full in all that is good and eternal. Where there were gaps in your life, losses
suffered, harm done, I have restored, comforted, forgiven you. In their place, I have revealed the gold
of wisdom and completeness to make you glad. Go and tell others what I have done, and can do for
them."

"Can two walk together, except they be agreed?" Amos 3:3

"For there are three that bear record in Heaven, the Father, the Word, and the Holy Ghost: and these three are one."
1 John 5:7

"Trust in the Lord with all your heart; and lean not unto your own understanding. In all your ways acknowledge Him, and He shall direct your paths." Proverbs 3:5-6

"Surely I have behaved and quieted myself, as a child that is weaned of his mother: my soul is even as a weaned child."
Psalm 131:2

"By agreement is how we journey together in power. You agree with My Word and My Spirit. Lay aside your own opinions and small understanding. I know the whole picture, and lead you through by wise step after wise step. You quiet yourself to receive My voice of security and peace."

February 14

"And this is His commandment, That we should believe on the Name of His Son Jesus Christ, and love one another, as He gave us commandment." 1 John 3:23

"No man has seen God at any time. If we love one another, God dwells in us, and His love is perfected in us."
1 John 4:12

"Therefore if any man be in Christ, he is a new creature: old things are passed away; behold, all things are become new."
11 Corinthians 5:17

"And hope makes not ashamed; because the love of God is shed abroad in our hearts by the Holy Ghost which is given unto us." Romans 5:5

"I am the giver of every good and perfect gift. I am the only source of perfection. Recognize Me in all the glory and signs around you. My joy is knowing you recognize Me in every new morning—new hope, new life energy, new gifts. Go, and allow My love to be spread abroad by My giving Spirit in you.
Love gives!

February 15

"All Scripture is given by inspiration of God, and is profitable for doctrine, for reproof, for correction, for instruction in righteousness: That the man of God may be perfect, throughly furnished unto all good works." II Timothy 3:16-17

"If you then be risen with Christ, seek those things which are above, where Christ sits on the right hand of God. Set your affections on things above, not on things of the earth." Colossians 3:1-2

"Wherefore come out from among them, and be you separate, says the Lord, and touch not the unclean thing; and I will receive you." II Corinthians 6:17

Jesus said, "I am the way, the truth, and the life: no man comes to the Father, but by Me." John 14:6

"Let Me be the central inspiration and motivation of your thoughts and behavior. In this, you must be diligent to discern and separate yourself from the influences of your culture and time. Set your love on Me and on things above. Therein lies the key to supernatural living, the ultimate, highest, most thrilling life possible—this is the way."

February 16

"Therefore I take pleasure in infirmities, in reproaches, in necessities, in persecutions, in distresses for Christ's sake: for when I am weak, then am I strong." II Corinthians 12:10

"Humble yourselves therefore under the mighty hand of God, that He may exalt you in due time: Casting all your care upon Him; for He cares for you." 1 Peter 5:6-7

Jesus said, "I am the vine, you are the branches: He that abides in Me, and I in him, the same brings forth much fruit: for without Me you can do nothing." John 15:5

"Whither shall I go from Your Spirit? or whither shall I flee from Your presence?" Psalm 139:7

"You are mine. No matter your weaknesses or failures. You are under My care. Accept that imperfections are human and real. You see more deeply your helplessness and your need for Me, your Heavenly Father. Escape from truth is never the answer."

February 17

"The heart is deceitful above all things, and desperately wicked: who can know it?" Jeremiah 17:9

"Let no man deceive himself. If any man among you seems to be wise in this world, let him become a fool, that he may be wise. For the wisdom of this world is foolishness with God. For it is written, He takes the wise in their own craftiness." 1 Corinthians 3:18-19

"And be not drunk with wine, wherein is excess; but be filled with the Spirit." Ephesians 5:18

"When You said, Seek you My face; my heart said unto You, Your face Lord will I seek." Psalm 27:8

"Do not be deceived by outer appearances, nor man's explanations. Be full of My Spirit, and see to the heart and true motive. Thereby, you know rightly how to respond and decide, and avoid confusion and pain. My people know My voice and are ever seeking Me in all things."

February 18

"And My people shall dwell in a peaceable habitation, and in sure dwellings, and in quiet resting places." Isaiah 32:18

"And I will give you the treasures of darkness, and hidden riches of secret places, that you may know that I, the Lord which call you by your name, am the God of Israel." Isaiah 45:3

"Woe to the rebellious children, says the Lord, that take counsel, but not of Me; and that cover with a covering, but not of My Spirit, that they may add sin to sin." Isaiah 30:1

"And it shall come to pass, that before they call, I will answer; and while they are yet speaking, I will hear." Isaiah" 65:24

"Rest, find it easy to take My rest. Come into the secret, quiet place wherever you are, and take My comfort. Many are the woes and commotion of the world, but you do not have to partake. This is not denial or escape. This is where you find answers, life and change."

February 19

"But He knows the way that I take: when He has tried me, I shall come forth as gold." Job 23:10

"Wherefore the law was our schoolmaster to bring us unto Christ, that we might be justified by faith." Galatians 3:24

"Know you not, that to whom you yield yourselves servants to obey, his servants you are to whom you obey; whether of sin unto death, or of obedience unto righteousness." Romans 6:16

"Blessed be God, even the Father of our Lord Jesus Christ, the Father of mercies, and the God of all comfort; who comforts us in all our tribulation, that we may be able to comfort them which are in any trouble, by the comfort wherewith we ourselves are comforted by God." II Corinthians 1:4

"When you are tried, and endure, you come forth as pure gold. Remember, your life is a school, whereby you learn from suffering and obedience who I am. Learn to love Me and My correction, and discipline yourself. Filled with My Spirit, you can come through trials, and help others come through."

February 20

"A bishop then must be blameless, the husband of one wife, vigilant, sober, of good behaviour, given to hospitality, apt to teach." 1 Timothy 3:2

"Use hospitality one to another without grudging." 1 Peter 4:9

"That there should be no schism in the body; but that the members should have the same care one for another."
1 Corinthians 12:25

"For all the promises of God in Him are yes, and in Him Amen, unto the glory of God by us." 1 Corinthians 1:20

"Your hospitality is an opportunity for Me to show Myself through your thoughtful attention to caring details and generosity. Let My love pour out wherever you can, and reveal how much I care for each individual's worth and needs. I am the yes and amen good Father to all."

February 21

Jesus said, "Take My yoke upon you, and learn of Me; for I am meek and lowly in heart: and you shall find rest unto your souls. For My yoke is easy, and My burden is light." Matthew 11:29-30

"Let your conversation be without covetousness; and be content with such things as you have: for He has said, I will never leave you nor forsake you." Hebrews 13:5

"That the blessing of Abraham might come on the Gentiles through Jesus Christ; that we might receive the promise of the Spirit through faith." Galatians 3:14

"Keep you heart with all diligence; for out of it are the issues of life." Proverbs 4:23

"Take My yoke upon you. Find contentment where I have placed you. Let My anointing oil cover you, and bring you to joyful acceptance. Abraham's great blessings are yours. Keep My peace, guard your heart."

February 22

"O Lord of hosts, blessed is the man that trusts in You." Psalm 84:12

Jesus said, "For verily I say unto you, That whosoever shall say unto this mountain, Be you removed, and be you cast into the sea; and shall not doubt in his heart, but shall believe that those things which he has said shall come to pass; he shall have whatsoever he says." Mark 11:23

"But speak you the things which become sound doctrine: That the aged men be sober, grave, temperate, sound in faith, in charity, in patience." Titus 2:1-2

"Blessed are the meek: for they shall inherit the earth." Matthew 5:5

"Trust My unfailing Spirit is with and in you. Cast off all doubt, worry, and fear. In your ever changing world, I am eternally unmoveable and sound. Blessed are the meek, for everything is available to them."

February 23

"Giving thanks unto the Father, which has made us meet to be partakers of the inheritance of the saints in light: Who has delivered us from the power of darkness, and has translated us into the Kingdom of His dear Son: in whom we have redemption through His blood, even the forgiveness of sins." Colossians 1:12-14

"For I reckon that the sufferings of this present time are not worthy to be compared with the glory which shall be revealed in us. Romans 8:18

"But now being made free from sin, and becoming servants to God, you have your fruit unto holiness, and the end everlasting life." Romans 6:22

"For they that are after the flesh do mind the things of the flesh; but they that are after the Spirit the things of the Spirit. For to be carnally minded is death; but to be spiritually minded is life and peace." Romans 8:5-6

"Take comfort in your forgiven sins, your transformed mind and your eternal glory with Me. At this time, you cannot comprehend the extent of My redemption. It's glory dims the sufferings and limitations of earthly life and makes them small indeed. I would have you glad, joyful, and thankful for Me, and for the benefit of others. You are called to lead as My servant, welcoming and attracting many to My arms and home. In all situations, it's your spirit that matters foremost."

February 24

"That He would grant you, according to the riches of His glory, to be strengthened with might by His Spirit in the inner man." Ephesians 3:16

"And the fruit of righteousness is sown in peace of them that make peace." James 3:18

Jesus said, *"But I say unto you, Love your enemies, bless them that curse you, do good to them that hate you, and pray for them which despitefully use you, and persecute you."* Matthew 5:44

Jesus said, *"Peace I leave with you, My peace I give unto you: not as the world gives, give I unto you. Let not your heart be troubled, neither let it be afraid."* John 14:27

"Maintain My inner peace in whatever circumstances that come. Trust My purpose, and find what I am doing. See the benefit that could come in every life and situation. Agree with Me to see it come to pass. Do not trouble yourself with every problem you encounter."

February 25

"Fear not; for you shall not be ashamed: neither be you confounded; for you shall not be put to shame: for you shall forget the shame of your youth, and shall not remember the reproach of your widowhood anymore." Isaiah 54:4

"...faith which works by love." Galatians 5:6

Jesus said, *"Verily I say unto you, whosoever shall not receive the Kingdom of God as a little child shall in no wise enter therein."* Luke 18:17

Jesus said, *"I am the light of the world: he that follows Me shall not walk in darkness, but shall have the light of life."* John 8:12

"All guilt and shame must be recognized and put aside when you follow Me. As you attune your spirit to Mine, I can direct and lead you. Faith works by love, not fear. Try to remember the trust of your childhood. This is the trust you must transfer to Me with joyful love and gratitude. I intend for My children to follow Me in wonder and true happiness."

February 26

"Follow after charity, and desire spiritual gifts, but rather that you may prophesy." 1 Corinthians 14:1

"Now concerning spiritual gifts, brethren, I would not have you ignorant." 1 Corinthians 12:1

"But the manifestation of the Spirit is given to every man to profit withal. For to one is given by the Spirit the word of wisdom; to another the word of knowledge by the same Spirit; to another faith by the same Spirit; to another the gifts of healing by the same Spirit; To another the working of miracles; to another prophesy; to another discerning of spirits; to another diverse kinds of tongues; to another the interpretation of tongues: But all these work that one and the selfsame Spirit, dividing to every man severally as He will." 1 Corinthians 12:7-11

"For we are laborers together with God: you are God's husbandry, you are God's building." 1 Corinthians 3:9

"Desire—greatly desire—My Spiritual gifts. You need these to fulfill your destiny. Receiving them by faith opens up your access to the supernatural power I make available to you. Your understanding of the reality of My Kingdom will increase as you co-labor with Me, using My gifts."

February 27

"And Jesus said, Somebody has touched Me: for I perceive that virtue has gone out of Me." Luke 8:46

"And He touched her hand, and the fever left her: and she arose, and ministered unto them." Matthew 8:15

Jesus said, "And these signs shall follow them that believe; In My Name....they shall lay hands on the sick, and they shall recover." Mark 16:17-18

Jesus said, "Suffer little children, and forbid them not, to come unto Me: for of such is the Kingdom of Heaven. And He laid His hands on them, and departed thence." Matthew 19:14-15

"Touch is very important to Me. I touch you, as you ask and need. Much is expressed wordlessly through a touch. Remember, My healing power came through My hands. I would that what comes through your hands would bring My healing, caring, affirming security to many. Touch others for Me."

February 28

"But you, beloved, building up yourselves on your most holy faith, praying in the Holy Ghost, Keep yourselves in the love of God, looking for the mercy of our Lord Jesus Christ unto eternal life." Jude 20-21

"Examine yourselves, whether you be in the faith; prove your own selves." II Corinthians 13:5

"Let your moderation be known unto all men." Philippians 4:5

"And what agreement has the temple of God with idols? For you are the temple of the living God; as God has said, I will dwell in them, and walk in them; and I will be their God, and they shall be My people. Wherefore come out from among them, and be you separate, says the Lord, and touch not the unclean thing: and I will receive you, And will be a Father unto you, and you shall be My sons and daughters, says the Lord Almighty." II Corinthians 6:16-18

"Build yourself up in your most holy faith. There is much that would want to tear you down. Even examining yourself can be overdone. Confess your sins and be free. Do not allow the sins and weaknesses of others to be projected on to you, and debilitate you with over questioning, criticizing, or over evaluating yourself. Be led of Me, and keep yourself separated from all unrighteousness."

February 29

"For what has man of all his labor, and of the vexation of his heart, wherein he has labored under the sun? For all his days are sorrows, and his travail grief; yes, his heart takes not rest in the night. This is also vanity." Ecclesiastes 2:22-23

"But what things were gain to me, those I counted loss for Christ. Yes, doubtless, and I count all things but loss for the excellency of the knowledge of Christ Jesus my Lord: for whom I have suffered the loss of all things, and do count them but dung, that I may win Christ." Philippians 3:7-8

"Wherefore let them that suffer according to the will of God commit the keeping of their souls to Him in well doing, as unto a faithful Creator." 1 Peter 4:19

"For Christ also has once suffered for sins, the just for the unjust, that He might bring us to God, being put to death in the flesh, but quickened by the Spirit." 1 Peter 3:18

"All men suffer, knowingly or unknowingly. There is a great difference between suffering with Me and suffering without Me—My fellowship and help. Suffering can teach, correct, and bring My life. Oh, that men would believe Me and My Word. Much suffering would be redemptive if only men would turn to Me, their Creator, first in all life's needs."

March

March 1

"I wait for the Lord, my soul does wait, and in His Word do I hope." Psalm 130:5

"Draw nigh to God, and He will draw nigh to you." James 4:8

Jesus said, "Yes rather, blessed are they that hear the Word of God, and keep it." Luke 11:28

"But without faith it is impossible to please Him: for he that comes to God must believe that He is, and that He is a rewarder of them that diligently seek Him." Hebrews 11:6

"Waiting, listening, drawing very close to Me is the most satisfying, sweet time of your day. It sets the pattern for all your time, as your spirit lingers close to Mine. Even as you go about your work day, I am in close fellowship, speaking as is needed. What could be more pleasing than this?"

March 2

"And He called unto Him the twelve, and began to send them forth by two and two; and gave them power over unclean spirits; And commanded them that they should take nothing for their journey, save a staff only; no scrip, no bread, no money in their purse: But be shod with sandals; and not put on two coats." Mark 6:7-9

Jesus said, "The harvest truly is great, but the laborers are few: pray you therefore the Lord of the harvest, that He would send forth laborers into His harvest." Luke 10:2

"Two are better than one; because they have a good reward for their labor." Ecclesiastes 4:9

"Faithful is He that calls you, who also will do it." 1 Thessalonians 5:24

Yes, I sent My disciples by two. Two are stronger than one alone. I still send My disciples by two today. When it is My plan, all will be in My order, and all that is needed will be provided. In these days, I have many places in mind for help and transformation. Where are the laborers that I may send? Allow Me to prepare you and lead you to those perfectly suited to your call and gifts."

March 3

"For you see your calling, brethren, how that not many wise men after the flesh, not many mighty, not many noble, are called: But God has chosen the foolish things of the world to confound the wise; and God has chosen the weak things of the world to confound the things which are mighty." 1 Corinthians 1:26-27

"Let this mind be in you, which was also in Christ Jesus." Philippians 2:5

Jesus said, "Wherefore I say unto you, Her sins, which are many, are forgiven; for she loved much: but to whom little is forgiven, the same loves little." Luke 7:47

Jesus said, "Blessed are the poor in spirit: for theirs is the Kingdom of Heaven." Matthew 5:3

"Yes, as you draw ever closer to Me, and think My thoughts, your imperfections, weaknesses, and sinfulness become clearer, more conscious, and failures hurt more. But, rejoice, for you are needing more of My forgiveness, strength, and wisdom. Blessed, loving, happy, are you, poor in spirit."

March 4

"And let us not be weary in well doing: for in due season we shall reap, if we faint not." Galatians 6:9

"Therefore with joy shall you draw water out of the wells of salvation." Isaiah 12:3

"Bless the Lord, O my soul, and forget not all His benefits: Who forgives all your iniquities; who heals all your diseases; who redeems your life from destruction; who crowns you with loving kindness and tender mercies; Who satisfies your mouth with good things; so that your youth is renewed like the eagle's." Psalm 103:2-5

"This is the day which the Lord has made; we will rejoice and be glad in it." Psalm 118:24

"Do not become weary in well doing. Serving is My honor for you. Draw strength and joy out of My endless wellspring of salvation. I've redeemed and saved you to give out of My riches. Take your rest in Me, and go on rejoicing to be used by Me."

March 5

"Watch you, stand fast in the faith, quit you like men, be strong." 1 Corinthians 16:13

"The law of the Lord is perfect; converting the soul: the testimony of the Lord is sure, making wise the simple." Psalm 19:7

"...you are the temple of the living God; as God has said, I will dwell in them, and walk in them; and I will be their God, and they shall be My people." II Corinthians 6:16

"For the Word of God is quick, and powerful, and sharper than any two-edged sword, piercing even to the dividing asunder of soul and spirit, and of the joints and marrow, and is a discerner of the thoughts and intents of the heart." Hebrews 4:12

"Instill My courageous faith by your living example. By acting on your steadfast belief in Me, and what I say, you show I am real, active, and always true to My Word. Nothing is lacking where true, brave hearts look to Me."

March 6

"Enter you in at the strait gate: for wide is the gate, and broad is the way, that leads to destruction, and many there be which go in thereat: Because strait is the gate, and narrow is the way, which leads unto life, and few there be that find it." Matthew 7:13-14

"If you be willing and obedient, you shall eat the good of the land." Isaiah 1:19

"The entrance of your words gives light; it gives understanding unto the simple." Psalm 119:130

Jesus said, "The thief comes not, but for to steal, and to kill, and to destroy: I am come that they might have life, and that they might have it more abundantly." John 10:10

"Obedience to Me and My way is not an ordeal, but a gateway to all the true pleasures man seeks. It's My will for you to savor and enjoy all the good I have created for you. But, when pleasure becomes your goal, sorrow and pain are sure to follow. The entry of My words into man, brings the life they desire. Your enemy would deceive you to rebel and be destroyed."

March 7

Jesus said, "Give, and it shall be given unto you; good measure, pressed down, and shaken together, and running over, shall men give into your bosom. For with the same measure that you mete withal it shall be measured to you again." *Luke 6:38*

Jesus said, "For unto whomsoever much is given, of him shall be much required." *Luke 12:48*

"But this I say, He which sows sparingly shall reap also sparingly; and he which sows bountifully shall reap also bountifully. Every man according as he purposes in his heart, so let him give; not grudgingly, or of necessity: for God loves a cheerful giver. And God is able to make all grace abound towards you; that you, always having all sufficiency in all things, may abound to every good work." *II Corinthians 9:6-8*

"Whereby are given unto us exceeding great and precious promises: that by these you might be partakers of the divine nature, having escaped the corruption that is in the world through lust." *II Peter 1:4*

"'Give, and it shall be given unto you, pressed down, running over.....' Yes, I command My children to be first, good givers. This goes against their nature, but in their obedience, they come to know My nature and My smile."

March 8

"With my whole heart have I sought You: O let me not wander from Your commandments." Psalm 119:10

"The angel of the Lord encamps round about them that fear Him, and delivers them." Psalm 34:7

"Have you not known? Have you not heard, that the everlasting God, the Lord, the Creator of the ends of the earth, faints not, neither is weary? There is no searching of His understanding. He gives power to the faint; and to them that have no might He increases strength." Isaiah 40:28-29

"If you will diligently hearken to the voice of the Lord your God, and will do that which is right in His sight, and will give ear to His commandments, and keep all His statutes, I will put none of these diseases upon you, which I have brought upon the Egyptians: for I am the Lord that heals you." Exodus 15:26

"Grant Me your heart's presence. Put aside all distractions. Experience Me surrounding you. So much that seems important now will fall away. I long to refresh My children in their weariness and cares. Turn to Me first, and not to man's devices and efforts to escape or mend. Remember, I am your healer."

March 9

"For this cause also thank we God without ceasing, because when you received the Word of God which you heard of us, you received it not as the word of men, but as it is in truth, the Word of God, which effectually works also in you that believe." 1 Thessalonians 2:13

"This is My beloved Son, in whom I am well pleased; hear you Him." Matthew 17:5

"Righteousness shall go before Him; and shall set us in the way of His steps." Psalm 85:13

Jesus said, *"I am among you as He that serves."* Luke 22:27

"My dear child, it pleases Me when you hear My Words and respond at once with My heart. Then, we are working together to accomplish great things, even in small steps and gestures. Be re-vitalized in your love to serve others in My Name."

March 10

"We are bound to thank God always for you, brethren, as it is meet, because that your faith grows exceedingly, and the charity of every one of you all toward each other abounds." II Thessalonians 1:3

"Let nothing be done through strife or vainglory; but in lowliness of mind let each esteem the other better than themselves." Philippians 2:3

Jesus said, "Fear not therefore, you are of more value than many sparrows." Matthew 10:31

"...for the Lord sees not as man sees; for man looks on the outward appearance, but the Lord looks on the heart." 1 Samuel 16:7

"Yes, look for the good, the growth in others. Let it be a starting place for love and esteeming others above yourself. No one can estimate the worth I place on one life. I look on the heart."

March 11

"He has made everything beautiful in His time: also He has set the world in their heart, so that no man can find out the work that God makes from the beginning to the end." Ecclesiastes 3:11

"But though He had done so many miracles before them, yet they believed not on Him." John 12:37

"The heavens declare the glory of God; and the firmament shows His handywork." Psalm 19:1

"He has filled the hungry with good things; and the rich He has sent empty away." Luke 1:53

"I am ever creating the new, and the beautiful, and the good. Much happens that is unseen, overlooked, and misunderstood by man. Only those who have eyes to see and ears to hear recognize My handiwork all around them continually. Truly, I create a feast for the hungry."

March 12

"But Godliness with contentment is great gain." 1 Timothy 6:6

Jesus said, "Whosoever therefore shall humble himself as this little child, the same is greatest in the Kingdom of Heaven." Matthew 18:4

"But He gives more grace. Wherefore He says, God resists the proud, but gives grace unto the humble." James 4:6

"He that is greedy of gain troubles his own house; but he that hates gifts shall live." Proverbs 15:27

"Dear child, be ever content with the humble simplicity of your childlike position. In this position, you are ever conscious of being under My all powerful, wise care. Grasping and controlling attitudes do not become My children, and do not bring My true gifts of righteousness, peace, and joy."

March 13

"For the Lord God is a sun and a shield: the Lord will give grace and glory: no good thing will He withhold from them that walk uprightly. Psalm 84:11

"If you walk in My statutes, and keep My commandments, and do them; Then I will give you rain in due season, and the land shall yield her increase, and the trees of the field shall yield their fruit." Leviticus 26:3-4

Jesus said, "If you then, being evil, know how to give good gifts unto your children: how much more shall your Heavenly Father give the Holy Spirit to them that ask Him?" Luke 11:13

"Then said Jesus unto His disciples, If any man will come after Me, let him deny himself, and take up his cross, and follow Me." Matthew 16:24

"As you know, I am a Father who will not withhold any good thing from those who walk uprightly with Me as My own children. However, it is My vast wisdom to know what is truly and ultimately that good thing. This, therefore, is the reason for man's often questioning and misunderstanding Me. The simple answer is to deny yourself, and embrace Me more completely. I do speak and reveal deeper truth to those willing to accept it."

March 14

"Deep calls unto deep at the noise of Your waterspouts: all Your waves and Your billows are gone over me." Psalm 42:7

"Daniel answered and said, Blessed be the Name of God forever and ever: for wisdom and might are His: And He changes the times and the seasons." Daniel 2:20

"And we know that all things work together for good to them that love God, to them who are the called according to His purpose." Romans 8:28

"David encouraged himself in the Lord his God." 1 Samuel 30:6

"My child, all the waves and billows shall not move you from your place in Me. Let new faith be established in your heart, that I have yet another new season for you. A season of greater restoration and peace, for I conclude all things well for those who love Me first, and in all situations. I am the great encourager."

March 15

"Train up a child in the way he should go: and when he is old, he will not depart from it." Proverbs 22:6

"For this is the covenant that I will make with the house of Israel after those days, says the Lord; I will put My laws into their mind, and write them in their hearts: and I will be to them a God, and they shall be to Me a people: And they shall not teach every man his neighbor, and every man his brother, saying, Know the Lord: for all shall know Me, from the least to the greatest." Hebrews 8:10-11

Jesus said, "I am the vine, you are the branches: He that abides in Me, and I in him, the same brings forth much fruit: for without Me you can do nothing." John 15:5

"And be not conformed to this world: but be you transformed by the renewing of your mind, that you may prove what is that good, and acceptable, and perfect, will of God." Romans 12:2

"It gives Me joy to train up My children to know, love, and serve Me. Many want to serve in avoidance of first knowing Me and knowing themselves. Without Me, service is burdensome and often fruitless. I came for your redemption and your individual transformation first. This is My order, and I know best."

March 16

"Casting down imaginations, and every high thing that exalts itself against the knowledge of God, and bringing into captivity every thought to the obedience of Christ." II Corinthians 10:5

"let us therefore cast off the works of darkness, and let us put on the armor of light." Romans 13:12

"the beloved of the Lord shall dwell in safety by Him; and the Lord shall cover him all the day long, and he shall dwell between His shoulders." Deuteronomy 33:12

"... and he went on his way rejoicing." Acts 8:39

"Dear one, cast down all imaginations that do not exalt Me. Take no care for real or imagined opinions and judgments of others. Allow Me to touch others in their needs and opinions. You go your way rejoicing, and be of good cheer as My humble child, beloved and protected."

March 17

"But Godliness with contentment is great gain." 1 Timothy 6:6

"For what has man of all his labor, and of the vexation of his heart, wherein he has labored under the sun? For all his days are sorrows, and his travail grief; yes, his heart takes not rest in the night. This is also vanity." Ecclesiastes 2:22-23

"Hell and destruction are never full; so the eyes of man are never satisfied." Proverbs 27:20

"I have longed for Your salvation, O Lord; and Your law is my delight." Psalm 119:174

"Contentment—real, steadfast contentment—is only found in knowing Me, your Creator. All other pursuits can bring temporary happiness that fades quickly. When you desire something new to satisfy a longing or need, come to Me first. Draw near, and ask of Me with a surrendered heart. There, you will always be nurtured, filled, delighted, and satisfied."

March 18

"Grace be to you, and peace, from God our Father, and from the Lord Jesus Christ." Ephesians 1:2

"He has made His wonderful works to be remembered: the Lord is gracious and full of compassion." Psalm 111:4

"The merciful man does good to his own soul." Proverbs 11:17

"If that which you have heard from the beginning shall remain in you, you also shall continue in the Son, and in the Father." 1 John 2:24

"Receive My grace and extend grace to others. Use the gift of mercy liberally. Leave the faults of others to Me, and receive My grace for yourself. My peace I give you for today's troubles. Continue on with Me, and trust when it seems nothing is changing for the better."

March 19

"He (Jesus) … saw a publican, named Levi, sitting at the receipt of custom: and He said unto him, Follow Me. And he left all, rose up, and followed Him." Luke 5:27-28

"I call heaven and earth to record this day against you, that I have set before you life and death, blessing and cursing: therefore choose life, that both you and your seed may live." Deuteronomy 30:19

Jesus said, "Take My yoke upon you, and learn of Me; for I am meek and lowly in heart: and you shall find rest unto your souls." Matthew 11:29

"And He spoke a parable unto them, Can the blind lead the blind: shall they not both fall into the ditch?" Luke 6:39

"I am leading because you invited Me to. You are learning to follow Me. This is the training all must choose. You naturally want to follow your own blind and selfish way. Believe that My way is the best for you. Learn the way of meekness and lowliness from Me."

March 20

"Blessed be the Lord, who daily loads us with benefits, even the God of our salvation. Selah." Psalm 68:19

"Blessed are you, when men shall hate you, and when they shall separate you from their company, and shall reproach you, and cast out your name as evil, for the Son of man's sake. Rejoice you in that day, and leap for joy: for, behold, your reward is great in Heaven: for in the like manner did their fathers unto the prophets." Luke 6:22-23

"Give to every man that asks of you; and of him that takes away your goods ask them not again." Luke 6:30

"But you, when you pray, enter into your closet, and when you have shut your door, pray to your Father which is in secret; and your Father which sees in secret shall reward you openly." Matthew 6:6

"Most of My gifts are unseen, unnoticed, and unappreciated. So you will find are yours when they are directed and given through Me. This is not the important concern for you. Be intimately related to Me in obedience, faithfulness, and generosity, in any way I direct. You will enjoy great, joyful fellowship with Me as you are unconcerned with recognition and reward. I will supply both in surprising ways to delight your soul."

March 21

"I exhort therefore, that, first of all, supplications, prayers, intercessions, and giving of thanks, be made for all men."
1 Timothy 2:1

"Wherefore He is able also to save them to the uttermost that come unto God by Him, seeing He ever lives to make intercession for them." Hebrews 7:25

"And there appeared an angel unto Him from Heaven, strengthening Him." Luke 22:43

Jesus said, "Even as the Son of man came not to be ministered unto, but to minister, and to give His life a ransom for many." Matthew 20:28

"Yes, a life of interceding and caring for My best for others is not the usual life on earth. But, this is My life; always standing before My Father for you, and the life of My servants. Even the angels know and care for human needs. Consider it a high calling, hidden, necessary and greatly rewarded to minister virtue to many."

March 22

"The Lord God is my strength, and He will make my feet like hinds feet, and He will make me to walk upon mine high places." Habakkuk 3:19

"For, behold, the darkness shall cover the earth, and gross darkness the people: but the Lord shall arise upon you, and His glory shall be seen upon you." Isaiah 60:2

"You are the light of the world. A city that is set on an hill cannot be hid." Matthew 5:14

"But they that wait upon the Lord shall renew their strength; they shall mount up with wings as eagles; they shall run, and not be weary; and they shall walk and not faint." Isaiah 40:31

"My child, let Me renew your strength and hope. Be not downcast at your weakness. Rise in My spirit and press on. These are days of gathering darkness, but I am calling and filling My people to be an even greater light. So, wait on Me, renew your strength, rise up, walk, run, conquer."

March 23

"That you put off concerning the former conversation the old man which is corrupt according to the deceitful lusts; and be renewed in the spirit of your mind." Ephesians 4:22-23

"The Lord knows the thoughts of man, that they are vanity." Psalm 94:11

"He has shown you, O man, what is good; and what does the Lord require of you, but to do justly, and to love mercy, and to walk humbly with your God?" Micah 6:8

"Are you not then partial in yourselves, and are become judges of evil thoughts?" James 2:4

"Grow higher, grow taller in your spirit, that you might gain My view, My thoughts. This comes by laying aside your personal ambitions and opinions. Have I not said, humble yourself, think more highly of others, and do not judge? I am the judge."

March 24

"Have you not known? Have you not heard, that the everlasting God, the Lord, the Creator of the ends of the earth, faints not, neither is weary? There is no searching of His understanding." Isaiah 40:28

"That Christ may dwell in your hearts by faith; that you, being rooted and grounded in love, may be able to comprehend with all saints what is the breadth, and length, and depth, and height; and to know the love of Christ which passes knowledge, that you might be filled with all the fullness of God." Ephesians 3:17-19

"Because that which may be known of God is manifest in them; for God has shown it unto them. For the invisible things of Him from the creation of the world are clearly seen, being understood by the things that are made, even His eternal power and Godhead; so that they are without excuse." Romans 1:19-20

"He shall call upon Me, and I will answer him: I will be with him in trouble; I will deliver him, and honor him." Psalm 91:15

"How do you come to know Me, your Creator? Someone introduces you, or you see Me in My creation, and know I am. Thereafter, it requires communication, and your faith and desire. I am available to all people. I alone know every language. When anyone speaks to Me, I reply. Learn to enjoy My Words, My companionship and My ongoing revelation of Myself. Know Me."

March 25

"And He that sat upon the throne said, Behold, I make all things new." Revelation 21:5

"Preach the Word; be instant in season, out of season; reprove, rebuke, exhort with all longsuffering and doctrine."
II Timothy 4:2

"And he shall be like a tree planted by the rivers of water, that brings forth his fruit in his season; his leaf also shall not wither; and whatsoever he does shall prosper." Psalm 1:3

"And of His fulness have all we received, and grace for grace." John 1:16

"Yes, to everything there is a season. I enjoy your seasons of growth. I want you to enjoy all your seasons as well. There is much adventure and drama in a life lived with, and for Me. As you mature in Me, you learn to balance a humble childlike faith with bold, immediate obedience. Look to Me steadily and not to your human limitations."

March 26

"Consider the lilies of the field, how they grow; they toil not, neither do they spin." Matthew 6:28

"For the vision is yet for an appointed time, but at the end it shall speak, and not lie: though it tarry, wait for it: because it will surely come, it will not tarry." Habakkuk 2:3

"But as for me, I will walk in mine integrity: redeem me, and be merciful unto me." Psalm 26:11

Jesus said, "If you can believe, all things are possible to him that believes." Mark 9:23

"Consider the lilies, patiently, quietly awaiting the right time to begin a new season. Your life is ongoing new seasons as well. Be quiet, and reflect on what I am doing and want to do. What I say is possible to those who welcome growth: changed by My Spirit. I am a redeeming, transforming Father God. Co-operate with Me. Do not resist My changing seasons of growth."

March 27

"The Lord has called me from the womb; from the bowels of my mother has He made mention of my name." Isaiah 49:1

Jesus said, "I will not leave you comfortless; I will come to you." John 14:18

"Behold, I have longed after Your precepts: quicken me in Your righteousness." Psalm 119:40

"Jesus answered, Verily, verily, I say unto you, Except a man be born again, he cannot see the Kingdom of God." John 3:5

"I am the constant, comforting companion for which man longs. Even in the womb, man finds comfort in Me, and seeks to regain it. Many try to find this comfort in earthly substitutes. This longing is only satisfied when My children come home to Me. Then, they enter true life in their whole being."

March 28

Jesus said, "The wind blows where it listeth, and you hear the sound thereof, but cannot tell whence it comes, and whither it goes: so is every one that is born of the Spirit." John 3:8

Jesus said, "Even so it is not the will of your Father which is in Heaven, that one of these little ones should perish." Matthew 18:14

"Wait on the Lord: be of good courage, and He shall strengthen your heart: wait, I say, on the Lord." Psalm 27:14

"I delight to do your will, O my God: yea, Your law is within my heart." Psalm 40:8

"Because of your belief in Me and your character, without even speaking, all those around you are touched and enhanced, even led to Me by your presence and My Spirit in you. Resist the inclination to belittle your influence and life impact. My children follow Me, and that is enough."

March 29

"Nay, in all these things we are more than conquerors through Him that loved us." Romans 8:37

"With the pure You will show yourself pure." Psalm 18:26

"Hide not Your face far from me; put not your servant away in anger: You have been my help; leave me not, neither forsake me, O God of my salvation." Psalm 27:9

"But if we walk in the light, as He is in the light, we have fellowship one with another, and the blood of Jesus Christ His Son cleanses us from all sin." 1 John 1:7

"Yes, I truly am an all conquering God. Blessed are the pure in heart who do see Me, all present, ever speaking, ever creating. To become pure in heart requires surrender to the painful truth of your helplessness in the face of sin, weakness, evil, and your need for a Savior. Then, I am free to come into you with a cleansing flood to rescue, restore, purify, and conquer. It's My joy to do this."

March 30

"Righteousness exalts a nation: but sin is a reproach to any people." Proverbs 14:34

"Even so then at this present time also there is a remnant according to the election of grace." Romans 11:5

"You shall have no other gods before Me." Exodus 20:3

"You are all the children of light, and the children of the day: we are not of the night, nor of darkness." 1 Thessalonians 5:5

"Righteousness does exalt a nation. It begins in the quiet decisions of a heart after Me. Remember, I always have a true remnant of My children who will not worship any other gods but Me. These keep My light bright for all those who are seeking Me and My righteousness. Keep a tranquil, wise, and thankful heart in the middle of unrighteousness."

March 31

"A merry heart makes a cheerful countenance." Proverbs 15:13

Jesus said, "He also that received seed among the thorns is he that hears the Word; and the care of this world, and the deceitfulness of riches, choke the Word, and he becomes unfruitful." Matthew 13:22

"And have put on the new man, which is renewed in knowledge after the image of Him that created him." Colossians 3:10

"But Jesus called them unto Him, and said, Suffer little children to come unto Me, and forbid them not: for of such is the Kingdom of God." Luke 18:16

"Receive a merry, joyful, overflowing heart. Let My love overtake all your cares and efforts. There is a time for refreshing. Don't pass it by, even as you carry out your duties and responsibilities. Notice how easily children delight in small things and laugh in fullness of joy."

April

April 1

"I have chosen the way of truth: Your judgments have I laid before me." Psalm 119:30

"Let all the earth fear the Lord: let all the inhabitants of the world stand in awe of Him." Psalm 33:8

"The fear of the Lord is the beginning of knowledge: but fools despise wisdom and instruction." Proverbs 1:7

"They shall all know Me, from the least of them unto the greatest of them, says the Lord." Jeremiah 31:34

"Have I not given you the ability to reason, understand, and choose? I have made you to be able to think as I do. In this, you must choose to make the highest good by seeking to know Me for yourself. By this, you come to hold Me in wonder and reverence. In this way is wisdom revealed."

April 2

"Behold a virgin shall be with child, and shall bring forth a son, and they shall call His name Emmanuel, which being interpreted is, God with us." Matthew 1:23

"Now then we are ambassadors for Christ." II Corinthians 5:20

"If any man serve Me, let him follow Me; and where I am, there shall also My servant be: if any man serve me, him will My Father honour." John 12:26

"For the Father loves the Son, and shows Him all things that Himself does: and He will show Him greater works than these, that you may marvel." John 5:20

"Yes, I am truly Emmanuel. I am with you. I rejoice in every victory. As you experience My transforming power, you become more like Me in character, and a stronger, clearer channel for My saving power to others. Find great satisfaction in being My ambassador and servant. Expect even greater works of restoration and salvation."

April 3

"For we are unto God a sweet savor of Christ, in them that are saved, and in them that perish." II Corinthians 2:15

"For the eyes of the Lord are over the righteous, and His ears are open to their prayers." 1 Peter 3:12

"I have found David the son of Jesse, a man after Mine own heart, which shall fulfill all Mine will." Acts 13:22

"Pray without ceasing." 1 Thessalonians 5:17

"Your life may seem to you as plodding, insignificant, and mundane. Not so, in My eyes, child. Wherever you are, at home or abroad, My Spirit sends a sweet fragrance and sheds light. You are My eyes and My heart among all peoples where I send you. The world looks for great accomplishments, but I look for a heart after Me in all of life. A heart continually Mine is true success and accomplishment."

April 4

"For all have sinned, and come short of the glory of God." Romans 3:23

"Wash me throughly from mine iniquity, and cleanse me from my sin. For I acknowledge my transgressions: and my sin is ever before me." Psalm 51:2-3

"Behold, happy is the man whom God corrects: therefore despise not the chastening of the Almighty: For He makes sore, and binds up: He wounds, and His hands make whole." Job 5:17-18

"Finally, be you all of one mind, having compassion one of another, love as brethren, be pitiful, be courteous." 1 Peter 3:8

"Yes, I am training My children through revelation of their sinful, unrighteous nature. As they face their true weakness and hopeless condition, they come to see My loving solutions, and develop a true compassion for all other men. Then, they become fit to serve and love."

April 5

"Surely I have behaved and quieted myself, as a child that is weaned of his mother: my soul is even as a weaned child."
Psalm 131:2

"And on the seventh day God ended His work which He had made; and He rested on the seventh day from all His work which He had made." Genesis 2:2

"Come unto Me, all you that labor and are heavy laden, and I will give you rest." Matthew 11:28

"And when He had sent the multitudes away, He went up into a mountain apart to pray: and when the evening was come, He was there alone." Matthew 14:23

"Quietness and rest is sometimes enough to sooth and heal your soul and body. I understand the demands of your life, and the cost to body and soul. Take needed time alone with Me where no demands on you are made. I too rested when I faced the great needs of life on earth. Your Heavenly Father says. 'Come away and rest in Me.'"

April 6

"For if we have been planted together in the likeness of His death, we shall be also in the likeness of His resurrection: knowing this, that our old man is crucified with Him, that the body of sin might be destroyed, that henceforth we should not serve sin." Romans 6:5-6

"I am crucified with Christ: nevertheless I live; yet not I, but Christ lives in me: and the life which I now live in the flesh I live by the faith of the Son of God, who loved me, and gave Himself for me." Galatians 2:20

"The Lord is not slack concerning His promise, as some men count slackness; but is longsuffering to us-ward, not willing that any should perish, but that all should come to repentance." II Peter 3:9

"And He said unto them, Go you into all the world, and preach the Gospel to every creature." Mark 16:15

"From your side of My crucifixion, you are able to see the great gift and opportunity I offer to all mankind. Now, all people have access to My Father through My Son-of-Man sacrifice. It is My will that none should perish. Go, and tell of My gift of salvation to mankind."

April 7

"That I may know Him, and the power of His resurrection, and the fellowship of His sufferings, being made conformable unto His death." Philippians 3:10

"Jesus said unto her, I am the resurrection, and the life: he that believes in Me, though he were dead, yet shall he live: And whosoever lives and believes in Me shall never die. Believe you this?" John 11:25-26

"Wherefore He is able also to save them to the uttermost that come unto God by Him, seeing He ever lives to make intercession for them." Hebrews 7:25

"And I sought for a man among them, that should make up the hedge, and stand in the gap before Me for the land, that I should not destroy it." Ezekiel 22:30

"Know Me in the power of My resurrection, and also My sufferings. In this way, you understand how it is on earth and in Heaven; how I have the power available for saving, freeing, healing, and restoring. You can be one serving, interceding in the gap."

April 8

"Wherefore come out from among them, and be you separate, says the Lord." II Corinthians 6:17

"But you are a chosen generation, a royal priesthood, an holy nation, a peculiar people; that you should show forth the praises of Him who has called you out of darkness into His marvelous light." 1 Peter 2:9

"...but God forbid that I should glory, save in the Cross of our Lord Jesus Christ, by Whom the world is crucified unto me, and I unto the world." Galatians 6:14

Jesus said, "My Kingdom is not of this world." John 18:36

"Yes, you're called by My Name to be a separate and peculiar people. Not by any effort to be so, but because the attractions of the world have lost their power with you. Be comforted and content with the attractions of My Kingdom. My people have always been the minority."

April 9

"That you may be blameless and harmless, the sons of God, without rebuke, in the midst of a crooked and perverse nation, among whom you shine as lights in the world." Philippians 2:15

"And now abides faith, hope, charity, these three; but the greatest of these is charity." 1 Corinthians 13:13

"For I the Lord your God will hold your right hand, saying unto you, Fear not; I will help you." Isaiah 41:13

"Now unto Him that is able to do exceeding abundantly above all that we ask or think, according to the power that works in us, Unto Him be glory in the church by Christ Jesus throughout all ages, world without end. Amen." Ephesians 3:20-21

"Yes, as the sun is shining warmer and warmer, and brighter each day, so I would have you also shining My love stronger and stronger each day. You know My Spirit's power radiates stronger than all other powers. Fear not for the unknown future events and how to prepare for them. I am already prepared, and in your future."

April 10

"With my whole heart have I sought You: O let me not wander from Your commandments." Psalm 119:10

"Abraham believed God, and it was imputed unto him for righteousness: and he was called the friend of God." James 2:23

"For you see your calling, brethren, how that not many wise men after the flesh, not many mighty, not many noble, are called." 1 Corinthians 1:26

"Look unto Me, and be you saved, all the ends of the earth: for I am God, and there is none else." Isaiah 45:22

"Those who search for Me, their Heavenly Father and Friend, will find Me if their heart is sincere. Those who find Me, have a new call to turn and help those who are also seeking Me. I am a calling and supporting Father God. I reach to every corner of the earth through My own children, the humble and free."

April 11

"You therefore endure hardness, as a good soldier of Jesus Christ." II Timothy 2:3

"My times are in Your hand: deliver me from the hands of mine enemies, and from them that persecute me." Psalm 31:15

"Though He were a Son, yet learned He obedience by the things which He suffered." Hebrews 5:8

"For whom the Lord loves He chastens, and scourges every son whom He receives." Hebrews 12:6

"Hard times come. There's always something to be learned in hard times. Hard times precede good times in My Kingdom. Suffering makes a deep impression, and shows to the teachable how true is My Word. It's to be obeyed in love. I chasten those I love."

April 12

"He has remembered His covenant forever, the Word which He commanded to a thousand generations." Psalm 105:8

"For I am the Lord, I change not." Malachi 3:6

"Surely He scorns the scorners; but He gives grace unto the lowly." Proverbs 3:34

"For all the law is fulfilled in one word, even in this; You shall love your neighbor as yourself." Galatians 5:14

"I am a God of generations. One flows out of another. Much has been lost, turned, mixed, misunderstood, substituted, and forgotten through the ages. However, I do not change. I always come to the seeking, lowly ones and reveal Myself. This is the central fact; love Me, love My Word, love yourself, and love your neighbor. All else I give as needed by individuals."

April 13

Jesus Said, "It is written, My house shall be called the house of prayer." Matthew 21:13

"The meek will He guide in judgment: and the meek will He teach His way." Psalm 25:9

"For thus says the high and holy One that inhabits eternity, whose Name is Holy; I dwell in the high and holy place, with him also that is of a contrite and humble spirit, to revive the spirit of the humble, and to revive the heart of the contrite ones." Isaiah 57:15

"Delight yourself also in the Lord; and He shall give you the desires of your heart. Commit your way unto the Lord; trust also in Him; and He shall bring it to pass." Psalm 37:4-5

"My people are called to be a people of prayer. My house is a house of prayer. I teach you as you pray. I hear from the broken and contrite heart. I speak to the quiet, listening heart. I desire to fill My children. I am sufficient for every need and cry. I enjoy your dependent, close communion, and desire that you enjoy it also."

April 14

"He heals the broken in heart, and binds up their wounds." Psalm 147:3

"And let the peace of God rule in your hearts, to the which you also are called in one body; and be you thankful." Colossians 3:15

"Better is a little with righteousness than great revenues without right." Proverbs 16:8

"For you know the grace of our Lord Jesus Christ, that, though He was rich, yet for your sakes He became poor, that you through His poverty might be rich." II Corinthians 8:9

"A grateful heart towards Me is a healed, joyful heart. You find rest for your soul as you communicate with and listen to Me. In this way, a simple life grows deeper and richer in the real and important matters of human life."

April 15

"*And we know that the Son of God is come, and has given us an understanding, that we may know Him that is true, and we are in Him that is true, even in His Son Jesus Christ. This is the true God and eternal life.*" 1 John 5:20

"*But You, O Lord, are a God full of compassion, and gracious, longsuffering, and plenteous in mercy and truth.*" Psalm 86:15

"*For we know that the whole creation groans and travails in pain together until now.*" Romans 8:22

A Father of the fatherless, and a judge of the widows, is God in His holy habitation." Psalm 68:5

"Here at Eastertide on earth, many are thinking on Me as best they are able. Few know Me as I truly am, and take the time needed to know Me better. My compassion is ever flowing on My needy creation. I want to be known as the loving Father God."

April 16

"*That the trial of your faith, being much more precious than of gold that perishes, though it be tried with fire, might be found unto praise and honor and glory at the appearing of Jesus Christ.*" 1 Peter 1:7

"*Every man's work shall be made manifest: for the day shall declare it, because it shall be revealed by fire; and the fire shall try every man's work of what sort it is.*" 1 Corinthians 3:13

"*And now shall mine head be lifted up above mine enemies round about me: therefore will I offer in His tabernacle sacrifices of joy; I will sing, yes, I will sing praises unto the Lord.*" Psalm 27:6

"*If a man therefore purge himself from these, he shall be a vessel unto honor, sanctified, and meet for the master's use, and prepared unto every good work.*" II Timothy 2:21

"Yes, I allow the trials by fire to strengthen your faith for the times ahead; to show you what's in your heart, and to bring you to release and maturity. Don't look back to lesser times and comforts, but look ahead to greater rewards and sacrifices, with joy. It's My honor that you are My servant and messenger."

April 17

"The hope of the righteous shall be gladness." Proverbs 10:28

"The Lord by wisdom has founded the earth; by understanding has He established the heavens." Proverbs 3:19

"Teach me to do Your will; for You are my God: Your Spirit is good; lead me into the land of uprightness." Psalm 143:10

"For the Lord is good; His mercy is everlasting; and His truth endures to all generations." Psalm 100:5

"Gladly seek and follow My will. Surrender what you think you know. Acknowledge Me in all your ways. Receive from My infinite wisdom. Then, you will discover your life to be a story, an adventure of great meaning and significance. I only intend good for My children. My way may seem convoluted, indirect, and tedious, but I lead you through and around trouble and danger for your transformation. Will to allow Me, your Father, to use you, even when you don't understand, for My glorious, joyful outcomes."

April 18

Jesus said, "I am come that they might have life, and that they might have it more abundantly." John 10:10

"The wilderness and the solitary place shall be glad for them; and the desert shall rejoice, and blossom as the rose. It shall blossom abundantly, and rejoice even with joy and singing." Isaiah 35:1-2

"But my God shall supply all your need according to His riches in glory by Christ Jesus." Philippians 4:19

Jesus said, "You have not chosen Me, but I have chosen you, and ordained you, that you should go and bring forth fruit, and that your fruit should remain: that whatsoever you shall ask of the Father in My Name, He may give it to you." John 15:16

"Abundance, abundance, abundance. Even the word has a "dance" in it. Look around you. Every tree and flower is wondrously made in profusion. Am I not sufficient for every need? Be lifted up in joyful thanksgiving to be My chosen ones. I am God with you."

April 19

"Ask of Me, and I shall give you the heathen for your inheritance, and the uttermost parts of the earth for your possession." Psalm 2:8

"...for your Father knows what things you have need of, before you ask Him." Matthew 6:8

"Can two walk together, except they be agreed?" Amos 3:3

"For we are laborers together with God: you are God's husbandry, you are God's building." 1 Corinthians 3:9

"Ask of Me. Yes, you've even asked for nations to awaken, and I am answering. The small matters of your life are also important to Me. I hear your innermost needs and wants. Hear My innermost needs and wants. What joy when we agree and walk together. Rejoice in the great hope I give, and keep your longings in step with Mine. We work together."

April 20

The angel said, "He is not here, but is risen." Luke 24:6

"If you then be risen with Christ, seek those things which are above, where Christ sits on the right hand of God." Colossians 3:1

"And He that searches the hearts knows what is the mind of the Spirit, because He makes intercession for the saints according to the will of God." Romans 8:27

"For our light affliction, which is but for a moment, works for us a far more exceeding and eternal weight of glory." II Corinthians 4:17

"I am indeed risen and sitting with My Father. Your faith and trust in Me and My love open the way for Me to stand for you before My Father. This is life indeed. Have no care for the small blows that crucify your self. They bring the great weight of a glorious life with Me."

April 21

"For you, O Lord, are a God full of compassion, and gracious, longsuffering, and plenteous in mercy and truth."
Psalm 86:15

"When Simon Peter saw it, he fell down at Jesus' knees, saying, Depart from me; for I am a sinful man, O Lord."
Luke 5:8

*"Wherefore, He is able also to save them to the uttermost that come unto God by Him,
seeing He ever lives to make intercession for them."* Hebrews 7:25

*"Bless the Lord, O my soul, and forget not all His benefits: Who forgives all your iniquities; who heals all your diseases;
Who redeems your life from destruction; who crowns you with lovingkindness and tender mercies."* Psalm 103:2-4

"My forgiveness is a beautiful gift. When you face the truth of your rebellious nature against Me, you see your helplessness and hopelessness. All must face their true sinfulness before they treasure Me and My Cross required for their forgiveness. So, embrace Me, My child, confess your sins, and believe I am able to forgive to the uttermost. This is My lovingkindness to you."

April 22

"For I am the Lord, I change not." Malachi 3:6

*"But we all, with open face beholding as in a glass the glory of the Lord, are changed
into the same image from glory to glory, even as by the Spirit of the Lord."* II Corinthians 3:18

"And it shall come to pass afterward, that I will pour out My Spirit upon all flesh." Joel 2:28

Jesus, "a friend of publicans and sinners." Luke 7:34

"Yes, I lead on, unchanging, as you are changed, from glorious now, to glorious possibilities only I can think of and plan. These are days of great unrest, as My Spirit is poured over your earth. Many long for something to change their lives, not realizing that their longing is for Me. I have many characteristic titles, but you know Me as your Father God, friend to sinners."

April 23

"The earth is the Lord's, and the fullness thereof; the world, and they that dwell therein." Psalm 24:1

"I will remember the works of the Lord: surely I will remember Your wonders of old. I will meditate also on all Your work, and talk of Your doings." Psalm 77:11-12

"O sing unto the Lord a new song: sing unto the Lord all the earth." Psalm 96:1

"Let the people praise You, O God; let all the people praise you. Then shall the earth yield her increase; and God, even our own God, shall bless us." Psalm 67:5-6

"Can you feel the earth coming to life all around you again? This is as your response to My Spirit rouses you to new revelation. My work is ever new around and through you. You must recognize Me in it, agree with Me, and give the sacrifice of joyful praise."

April 24

"I will bless the Lord at all times: His praise shall continually be in my mouth." Psalm 34:1

"For whatsoever is born of God overcomes the world: and this is the victory that overcomes the world, even our faith." 1 John 5:4

"For I am persuaded, that neither death, nor life, nor angels, nor principalities, nor powers, nor things present, nor things to come, nor height, nor depth, nor any other creature, shall be able to separate us from the love of God, which is in Christ Jesus our Lord." Romans 8:38-39

"Behold, I will do a new thing; now it shall spring forth; shall you not know it? I will even make a way in the wilderness, and rivers in the desert." Isaiah 43:19

"Can you see how I bring you through times and seasons that want to discourage and destroy you? This is My overcoming victory, as you hold fast to Me and My Words. Nothing can separate you from Me, your hope. Continue in humility and watchfulness, as I bring new life in new seasons you have not imagined."

April 25

"For them that honour Me them will I honour." 1 Samuel 2:30

"Know you not that you are the temple of God, that the Spirit of God dwells in you?" 1 Corinthians 3:16

"But if you have bitter envying and strife in your hearts, glory not, and lie not against the truth." James 3:14

"Create in me a clean heart, O God; and renew a right spirit within me." Psalm 51:10

"I honor those who honor Me. I live by My Spirit in you, My temple. I cannot abide with pride, envy, and suspicion. Cast these out, that My Spirit has free flow. Recognize when a cleansing is needed. I will create in you a clean heart and renew a right spirit within you."

April 26

Jesus said, "Marvel not that I said unto you, you must be born again." John 3:7

"Therefore as by the offence of one judgment came upon all men to condemnation; even so by the righteousness of one the free gift came upon all men unto justification of life." Romans 5:18

"Blessed is the man whom You choose, and cause to approach unto You, that he may dwell in Your courts: we shall be satisfied with the goodness of Your house, even of Your holy temple." Psalm 65:4

Jesus said, "I am the door: by Me if any man enter in, he shall be saved, and shall go in and out, and find pasture." John 10:9

"The new birth is a reality. You become a renewed person when your spirit comes alive, rightly related to Me through My Son Jesus. The simplicity of this experience is available and free to all people. It is the first important decision needed to know Me, and your purpose and destiny on earth. My great love has provided this door, and would that all be saved through it."

April 27

"It is God that girds me with strength, and makes my way perfect." Psalm 18:32

"But the path of the just is as the shining light, that shines more and more unto the perfect day." Proverbs 4:18

"He that follows after righteousness and mercy finds life, righteousness, and honour." Proverbs 21:21

"He has shown you, O man, what is good; and what does the Lord require of you, but to do justly, and to love mercy, and to walk humbly with your God?" Micah 6:8

"My dear child, do not be excessively critical of yourself. Your pursuit of perfection is not Mine. I look to your heart that so much wants to be just with others and do what is right for them. This is part of your gift of mercy and desire for righteousness. You must leave others to Me. Do only what I direct, and have rest in Me for them and for yourself. Your first purpose is not to work for Me, but to work gently with Me."

April 28

"It is of the Lord's mercies that we are not consumed, because His compassions fail not. They are new every morning: great is Your faithfulness." Lamentations 3:22-23

"But I will sing of Your power; yes, I will sing aloud of Your mercy in the morning: for You have been my defence and refuge in the day of my trouble." Psalm 59:16

Jesus said, "Take therefore no thought for the morrow: for the morrow shall take thought for the things of itself. Sufficient unto the day is the evil thereof." Matthew 6:34

"Casting all your care upon Him; for He cares for you." 1 Peter 5:7

"Yes, receive My mercies anew every morning. All you have is today, to experience life with Me. Receive today's gift simply, without the complications of looking back with regrets. Today's troubles will be sufficient. The world is truly in My hands of care."

April 29

"When my father and my mother forsake me, then the Lord will take me up." Psalm 27:10

"O the depth of the riches both of the wisdom and knowledge of God! How unsearchable are His judgments, and His ways past finding out." Romans 11:33

"For God gives to a man that is good in His sight wisdom, and knowledge, and joy." Ecclesiastes 2:26

"That He would grant you, according to the riches of His glory, to be strengthened with might by His spirit in the inner man." Ephesians 3:16

"I am the Great Parent, the One who teaches how to nurture. I am the source of all knowledge and wisdom. I am a generous giver to all who truly ask and seek Me. My gifts are of priceless value, and bring all the riches in Christ, My Son."

April 30

Jesus said, "And I know that His commandment is life everlasting: whatsoever I speak therefore, even as the Father said unto Me, so I speak." John 12:50

"Know you that the Lord He is God: it is He that has made us, and not we ourselves; we are His people, and the sheep of His pasture." Psalm 100:3

"He is despised and rejected of men; a man of sorrows, and acquainted with grief: and we hid as it were our faces from Him; He was despised, and we esteemed Him not." Isaiah 53:3

"Blessed is the man that walks not in the counsel of the ungodly, nor stands in the way of sinners, nor sits in the seat of the scornful. But his delight is in the law of the Lord; and in His law does he meditate day and night." Psalm 1:1-2

"I am always communicating with My creation. Some understand and want to know Me more. Many accept flawed understanding or rejection of Me from others. I sent My Son Jesus so all could know Me as I truly am. Reckon yourself exceedingly blessed to know Me, and grow in that knowledge through My dear, perfect Son."

May

May 1

"For he that is entered into His rest, he also has ceased from his own works, as God did from His." Hebrews 4:10

"But when you shall hear of wars and commotions, be not terrified; for these things must first come to pass; but the end is not by and by." Luke 21:9

"One thing have I desired of the Lord, that will I seek after; that I may dwell in the house of the Lord all the days of my life, to behold the beauty of the Lord, and to inquire in His temple." Psalm 27:4

Jesus said, "Let not your heart be troubled: you believe in God, believe also in Me." John 14:1

"Rest, trust, obey, be at peace in Me. Though the world shakes with wars and need and unrest in many places, there is peace in My Kingdom. Enter deep into your spirit and find My order, beauty, and harmony. Let not your heart be troubled, My child."

May 2

Jesus said, "What therefore God has joined together, let not man put asunder." Matthew 19:6

"God sets the solitary in families." Psalm 68:6

"For what the law could not do, in that it was weak through the flesh, God sending His own Son in the likeness of sinful flesh, and for sin, condemned sin in the flesh." Romans 8:3

God, "Which does great things past finding out; yes, and wonders without number." Job 9:10

"I am a builder of relationships. I sent My Son to build relationships. Family is My idea. Creating, multiplying, unfolding, and growing is how I reveal Myself. Love is an inadequate word for Me and My desire for you. I am infinite; My thoughts and plans are past your human comprehension. In eternity, much will be better understood by you."

May 3

Jesus said, "And when you stand praying, forgive, if you have ought against any: that your Father also which is in Heaven may forgive you your trespasses." Mark 11:25

"A man's pride shall bring him low: but honour shall uphold the humble in spirit." Proverbs 29:23

Jesus said, "But the Comforter, which is the Holy Ghost, whom the Father will send in My Name, He shall teach you all things, and bring all things to your remembrance, whatsoever I have said unto you." John 14:26

Jesus said, "Because straight is the gate, and narrow is the way, which leads unto life, and few there be that find it." Matthew 7:14

"True forgiveness comes with My Divine Nature in you. When you decide to let self, pride, and judgment of others die, then My merciful nature fills their place. My Spirit in you is ever teaching, cleansing, and refining. This is the true school through which My children progress. Welcome My Spirit of revelation, and be led in the joy of all truth. This is the narrow and best path I have ordained."

May 4

"For You have been a strength to the poor, a strength to the needy in his distress, a refuge from the storm, a shadow from the heat, when the blast of the terrible ones is as a storm against the wall." Isaiah 25:4

"How excellent is Your lovingkindness, O God! Therefore the children of men put their trust under the shadow of Your wings." Psalm 36:7

"Grace and peace be multiplied unto you through the knowledge of God, and of Jesus our Lord. According as His divine power has given unto us all things that pertain unto life and Godliness, through the knowledge of Him that has called us to glory and virtue." II Peter 1:2-3

Jesus said, "But when the Comforter is come, whom I will send unto you from the Father, even the Spirit of truth, which proceeds from the Father, He shall testify of Me." John 15:26

"Weather the storms. Come under My sheltering wings as a child runs to its mother. Learn to quiet yourself. Recognize Me in the simple gestures, events, and things I provide. I sent the Comforter, as I knew the need you would have when troubles come."

"And the Lord shall guide you continually, and satisfy your soul in drought, and make fat your bones: and you shall be like a watered garden, and like a spring of water, whose waters fail not." Isaiah 58:11

"My Beloved has gone down into His garden, to the beds of spices, to feed in the gardens, and to gather lilies." Song of Solomon 6:2

"That He would grant you, according to the riches of His glory, to be strengthened with might by His Spirit in the inner man." Ephesians 3:16

"O worship the Lord in the beauty of holiness: fear before Him, all the earth." Psalm 96:9

"Altogether lovely is your inner garden where I preside. Enter in and enjoy refreshing time with Me. Speaking is not essential. A quiet exchange of love and gratitude is enough. I make your inner life fresh daily. Breathe in My presence and receive the beauty of holiness."

May 6

"He has made the earth by His power, He has established the world by His wisdom, and has stretched out the heavens by His discretion." Jeremiah 10:12

"From the rising of the sun unto the going down of the same the Lord's Name is to be praised." Psalm 113:3

"You are the God that does wonders: You have declared Your strength among the people." Psalm 77:14

"And on My servants and on My handmaidens I will pour out in those days of My Spirit; and they shall prophesy." Acts 2:18

"Do I not hold the earth together, and cause it to turn around by day and night? O, that the world would recognize My hand of power and control. Each new turn to the sun by morning is My love appearing to all. Reflect on My provision, and the wonders within you and without. I desire for you to know Me, and know My purpose for your life. All I do has My loving purposes in mind."

May 7

"Submit yourselves therefore to God. Resist the devil, and he will flee from you." James 4:7

Jesus said, "These things I have spoken unto you, that in Me you might have peace. In the world you shall have tribulation: but be of good cheer; I have overcome the world." John 16:33

"The heart is deceitful above all things, and desperately wicked: who can know it?" Jeremiah 17:9

"Follow peace with all men, and holiness, without which no man shall see the Lord: Looking diligently lest any man fail of the grace of God; lest any root of bitterness springing up trouble you, and thereby many be defiled." Hebrews 12:14-15

"Resist the enemy, and he will flee from you. Overcome your emotions, and respond from your spirit. Don't be deceived to linger in deceptive feelings or imaginations. Extend mercy and compassion to those who may hurt you. Don't linger in self-pity, resentment, and wrong thoughts."

May 8

"Remember Abraham, Isaac and Israel, Your servants, to whom You swore by Your own self, and said unto them, I will multiply your seed as the stars of heaven, and all this land that I have spoken of will I give unto your seed, and they shall inherit it forever." Exodus 32:13

"Now He that ministers seed to the sower both minister bread for your food, and multiply your seed sown, and increase the fruits of your righteousness." II Corinthians 9:10

"Now unto Him that is able to do exceeding abundantly above all that we ask or think, according to the power that works in us, Unto Him be glory in the church by Christ Jesus throughout all ages, world without end. Amen." Ephesians 3:20-21

"And He took the seven loaves and the fishes, and gave thanks, and broke them, and gave to His disciples, and the disciples to the multitude." Matthew 15:36

"I am the great multiplier. I take the small gifts and disperse them to multitudes. You cannot see, nor imagine how I continually use your actions, thoughts and words to build My church. When you generously, trustingly yield your all to Me, I send it out across the universe to have more influence than you can imagine. Thereby am I glorified by your life surrendered and given out for Me and the nurture of others."

May 9

"But the fruit of the Spirit is love, joy, peace, longsuffering, gentleness, goodness, faith, meekness, temperance: against such there is no law. And they that are Christ's have crucified the flesh with the affections and lusts. If we live in the Spirit, let us also walk in the Spirit." Galatians 5:22-25

"But put you on the Lord Jesus Christ, and make not provision for the flesh, to fulfill the lusts thereof." Romans 13:14

"There is therefore now no condemnation to them which are in Christ Jesus, who walk not after the flesh, but after the Spirit." Romans 8:1

"But Jesus said unto him, Follow Me." Matthew 8:22

"Self-control is essential to following Me. Walk in the Spirit, My only Holy Spirit, and you need not fulfill the lusts of the flesh."

May 10

"The mountains shall bring peace to the people, and the little hills, by righteousness." Psalm 72:3

"Yes, though I walk through the valley of the shadow of death, I will fear no evil: for You are with me; Your rod and Your staff they comfort me." Psalm 23:4

"Watch you therefore, and pray always, that you may be accounted worthy to escape all these things that shall come to pass, and to stand before the Son of Man." Luke 21:36

"For I the Lord your God will hold your right hand, saying unto you, Fear not; I will help you." Isaiah 41:13

"There are mountains, valleys and plains when you follow Me. Linger in each only as long as the lessons require. Look to what is needful in yourself. Watch and listen for what I am saying in every state you find yourself in. Guard your heart. Maintain a steady hold on Me, seeing what I might lead you to do for another. This keeps your self life in My order, and your thinking right, calm and joyful."

May 11

Jesus said, "My grace is sufficient for you: for My strength is made perfect in weakness." II Corinthians 12:9

"for the joy of the Lord is your strength." Nehemiah 8:10

Charity "Rejoices not in iniquity, but rejoices in the truth; Bears all things, believes all things, hopes all things, endures all things." 1 Corinthians 13:6-7

"For the Lamb which is in the midst of the throne shall feed them, and shall lead them unto living fountains of waters: and God shall   wipe away all tears from their eyes." Revelation 7:17

"Reckon on My grace being sufficient, and My joy to strengthen you. I am your source. Press on forward, directing your thoughts on My unfailing goodness, and let living waters flow from you. This is all that is needful."

May 12

"Then the king made Daniel a great man, and gave him many great gifts, and made him ruler over the whole province of Babylon, and chief of the governors over all the wise men of Babylon." Daniel 2:48

"And with many such parables spoke He the Word unto them, as they were able to hear it. But without a parable spoke He not unto them: and when they were alone, He expounded all things to His disciples." Mark 4:33-34

"Now no chastening for the present seems to be joyous, but grievous: nevertheless afterward it yields the peaceable fruit of righteousness unto them which are exercised thereby." Hebrews 12:11

Jesus said, "The harvest truly is great, but the laborers are few: pray you therefore the Lord of the harvest, that He would send forth labourers into His harvest." Luke 10:2

"Remember Daniel? He stood fast in Me, his God, in the midst of a seemingly all powerful culture. Those I love and use, I call to a greater discipline and knowledge of Me. It may at times seem a great hardship, but My correction, direction and selection are part of whom I've called you to be, and will eventually yield, not only the peaceable fruit of righteousness, but the purposes and harvest and destinies I intend."

May 13

Jesus said, "But I say unto you, Love your enemies, bless them that curse you, do good to them that hate you, and pray for them which despitefully use you, and persecute you." Matthew 5:44

"Trust in the Lord with all your heart; and lean not unto your own understanding. In all your ways acknowledge Him, and He shall direct your paths." Proverbs 3:5-6

"Study to show yourself approved unto God, a workman that needs not to be ashamed, rightly dividing the Word of truth." II Timothy 2:15

"Therefore with joy shall you draw water out of the wells of salvation." Isaiah 12:3

"You are called, with My guidance and self-control, to do others good. Not leaning to your understanding, but leaning on Me who knows what is best for each one. This is a life long learning. Be willing to be a good student. Communicating with, and turning your inner ear and heart to Me, is the beginning of a wondrous, deepening, rich life."

May 14

"For I am the Lord, I change not." Malachi 3:6

Jesus said, "And everyone that hears these sayings of mine, and does them not, shall be likened unto a foolish man, which built his house upon the sand." Matthew 7:26

"Except the Lord build the house, they labor in vain that build it: except the Lord keep the city, the watchman wakes but in vain." Psalm 127:1

"Charge them that are rich in this world, that they be not high minded, nor trust in uncertain riches, but in the living God, who gives us richly all things to enjoy." II Timothy 6:17

"There is no permanence outside of Me. Denial and disappointment are inevitable for those whose life is not built upon Me. Your faith in Me is a precious gift that sustains you and increases with exercise. Enjoy the faith life with Me. Revel in the adventure of the ever changing world experience while you are grounded in Me."

May 15

"And being in Bethany in the house of Simon the leper, as He sat at meat, there came a woman having an alabaster box of ointment of spikenard very precious; and she broke the box, and poured it on His head." Mark 14:3

"Finally, be you all of one mind, having compassion one of another, love as brethren, be pitiful, be courteous." 1 Peter 3:8

"Thus speaks the Lord of hosts, saying, Execute true judgment, and show mercy and compassion every man to his brother." Zechariah 7:9

Jesus said, "Truly, truly, I say unto you, Except a corn of wheat fall into the ground and die, it abides alone: but if it die, it brings forth much fruit." John 12:24

"Dear child, I see your sacrificial life poured out for others, always seeking what is right, what is just, what is needed. I have given you a heart of mercy and compassion. Go on gently, untroubled when others misunderstand you and your life. Rejoice that you are Mine, and much fruit is being born where it cannot be seen."

May 16

"But seek you first the Kingdom of God, and His righteousness; and all these things shall be added unto you."
Matthew 6:33

Jesus said, "Truly I say unto you, whosoever shall not receive the Kingdom of God as a little child, he shall not enter in."
Mark 10:15

Jesus said, "Children, how hard is it for them that trust in riches to enter into the Kingdom of God!" Mark 10:24

"All Your works shall praise You, O Lord; and Your saints shall bless You. They shall speak
of the glory of Your Kingdom, and talk of Your power; To make known to the sons of men
His mighty acts, and the glorious majesty of His Kingdom." Psalm 145:10-12

"Those who live in My Kingdom are satisfied, and laughter comes easy to them. Watch happy children at play, and see how the tiniest thing or event brings instant interest, joy, and laughter. In My Kingdom, there is continuous revelation of the new, unexpected, and glorious. This is why I said you must be as a little child to enter in and experience it. Did I not make available this abundant life to My children?"

May 17

"This is the day which the Lord has made; we will rejoice and be glad in it." Psalm 118:24

"Like as a father pities his children, so the Lord pities them that fear Him. For He knows our frame; He remembers that we are dust." Psalm 103:13-14

"The Lord is my portion, says my soul; therefore will I hope in Him. The Lord is good unto them that wait for Him, to the soul that seeks Him." Lamentations 3:24-25

"My soul, wait you only upon God; for my expectation is from Him. He only is my rock and my salvation: He is my defence; I shall not be moved." Psalm 62:5-6

"Each day is a fresh, new beginning with Me. Go forward full of joyful anticipation of what we will experience and do together. Know that I hear your prayers and see your dreams, and I reply and order responses. Be confident, I forget not you and your needs and hopes. It is My Fatherly joy to protect and provide all for My children."

May 18

Jesus said, "Judge not, that you be not judged. For with what judgment you judge, you shall be judged: and with what measure you mete, it shall be measured to you again." Matthew 7:1-2

Jesus said, "I am come a light into the world, that whosoever believes on Me should not abide in darkness. And if any man hear My Words, and believe not, I judge him not: for I came not to judge the world, but to save the world." John 12:46-47

Jesus said, "The first of all the commandments is, Hear, O Israel; the Lord our God is one Lord: And you shall love the Lord your God with all your heart, and with all your soul, and with all your mind, and with all your strength: this is the first commandment. And the second is like, namely this, You shall love your neighbor as yourself. There is none other commandment greater than these." Mark 12:29-31

Jesus said, "For if you forgive men their trespasses, your Heavenly Father will also forgive you: But if you forgive not men their trespasses, neither will your Father forgive your trespasses." Matthew 6:14-15

"Those sins, faults, failures, and weaknesses that you might judge and reject in others, indicate your need to examine all the potential for them in yourself. When you judge and reject others, that judgment will return to you in some way. My Word says to love your neighbor as yourself. Acknowledge your own real unrighteousness, and you can judge noone. This is a lesson long, and often painfully, learned. The fruit is to experience great mercy, compassion and love for all as I do. Forgiveness of self and others is a daily necessity."

May 19

"And suddenly there was with the angel a multitude of the Heavenly host praising God, and saying, Glory to God in the highest, and on earth peace, good will toward men." Luke 2:13-14

"While we look not at the things which are seen, but at the things which are not seen: for the things which are seen are temporal; but the things which are not seen are eternal." II Corinthians 4:18

"Remembering without ceasing your work of faith, and labour of love, and patience of hope in our Lord Jesus Christ, and in the sight of God and our Father." 1 Thessalonians 1:3

"If you then, being evil, know how to give good gifts unto your children, how much more shall your Father which is in Heaven give good things to them that ask Him?" Matthew 7:11

"I am the God of suddenly. It may appear that nothing is changing for long periods of time. Yet, I am at work in the unseen Spirit, and directing many situations. Then, suddenly, circumstances turn and you see new vistas and transformations. Remember, patience results from deep trust and communion with My Spirit. Your focus then is on Me, and less on your circumstances. I love to surprise My children."

May 20

Jesus said, "I am the bread of life: he that comes to Me shall never hunger; and he that believes on Me shall never thirst." John 6:35

"O taste and see that the Lord is good: blessed is the man that trusts in Him." Psalm 34:8

"For the bread of God is He which comes down from Heaven, and gives life unto the world." John 6:33

Jesus said, "It is written, That man shall not live by bread alone, but by every Word of God." Luke 4:4

"Break the bread of My Word into pieces suitable for the need. Hand it out with gentleness and mercy. Share, as you chew it yourself, and show how delicious and satisfying it is. Thus, you create more of a hunger for My truth. Declare how real and important My Words are to you. They are your very life, meeting every need, making daily life rich, joyful, and generous."

May 21

"If you be willing and obedient, you shall eat the good of the land." Isaiah 1:19

Jesus said, "I am the way, the truth, and the life: no man comes unto the Father, but by Me." John 14:6

Jesus said, "Enter you in at the strait gate: for wide is the gate, and broad is the way, that leads to destruction, and many there be which go in thereat: Because strait is the gate, and narrow is the way, which leads unto life, and few there be that find it." Matthew 7:13-14

Jesus said, "You are My friends, if you do whatsoever I command you." John 15:14

"Obedience is neither a hard, unpleasant way, nor one that shows off one's goodness. True obedience comes from right relationship in communing with Me, and a trust that I am the way, and My way is the best. Go gently and quietly with Me in all your everyday duties. Remember, My closest friends are often the obscure, unnoted, and most free."

May 22

Jesus said, "The Spirit of the Lord is upon Me, because He has anointed Me to preach the Gospel to the poor; He has sent Me to heal the broken hearted, to preach deliverance to the captives, and recovery of sight to the blind, to set at liberty them that are bruised, To preach the acceptable year of the Lord." Luke 4:18-19

"Bless the Lord, O my soul, and forget not all His benefits: Who forgives all your iniquities; who heals all your diseases; who redeems your life from destruction; who crowns you with loving kindness and tender mercies." Psalm 103:2-4

"...for I the Lord your God am a jealous God, visiting the iniquity of the fathers upon the children unto the third and fourth generation of them that hate Me." Exodus 20:5

"For I am not ashamed of the Gospel of Christ: for it is the power of God unto salvation to every one that believes; to the Jew first, and also to the Greek." Romans 1:16

"What is healing but a restoration of My original intent. Understand that sin affects all that it touches, seen and unseen. Much of what you cannot understand of suffering is the reaping of sin and its multiplied repercussions, often through generations. Ignorance of, and rejection of Me, intensify these consequences. Conviction of sin and repentance, with forgiveness, are My gift to begin healing and restoring My children. O, that the world would believe Me, My Son, and My Spirit."

May 23

"And they overcame him by the blood of the Lamb, and by the word of their testimony; and they loved not their lives unto death." Revelation 12:11

"Stand fast therefore in the liberty wherewith Christ has made us free, and be not entangled again with the yoke of bondage." Galatians 5:1

Jesus said, "If the Son therefore shall make you free, you shall be free indeed." John 8:36

"Righteousness exalts a nation: but sin is a reproach to any people." Proverbs 14:34

"Many have given, and many more will give the ultimate sacrifice to keep the freedom that only comes from Me. My Son and My Word give what every man and every nation need to bring peace and prosperity. O, if only My poor, hurting world would choose My saving love extended."

May 24

"Be not overcome of evil, but overcome evil with good." Romans 12:21

"For He satisfies the longing soul, and fills the hungry soul with goodness." Psalm 107:9

"I will instruct you and teach you in the way which you should go: I will guide you with My eye." Psalm 32:8

"Peter therefore was kept in prison: but prayer was made without ceasing of the church unto God for him." Acts 12:5

"Do not become overwhelmed by the needs and lack that you see around you. Reckon on your Father's abundance. My eyes see all. I await the hearts of men to awake to My reality and goodness. Each is able to accomplish much more than they imagine. Steward and release what I give you as My Spirit directs. It is an easy labor when you allow Me to direct every part of your life. Pray without ceasing and obey My voice."

May 25

"Fear you not therefore, you are of more value than many sparrows." Matthew 10:31

"What man is he that fears the Lord? Him shall He teach in the way that He shall choose." Psalm 25:12

"For the wages of sin is death; but the gift of God is eternal life through Jesus Christ our Lord." Romans 6:23

"As for God, His way is perfect: the Word of the Lord is tried: He is a buckler to all those that trust in Him." Psalm 18:30

"You observe the birds. They know how to find sustenance and shelter, and travel great distances. They craft strong, protected homes. Their young arrive in season. They follow Me as I created the life in them. So, it is with you. I created you with a specific destiny and life energy to follow it. You have the capacity to choose to use your life energy to follow My destiny plan. Too often, men choose to use My gifts and life energy to follow wrong paths, and blame Me for the ongoing disastrous consequences. My way is narrow, simple, and blessed. My voice of loving direction and help is available to whosoever wills to know Me through My dear Son Jesus."

May 26

"Charity never fails." 1 Corinthians 13:8

Jesus said, *"That you may be the children of your Father which is in Heaven: for He makes His sun to rise on the evil and on the good, and sends rain on the just and on the unjust."* Matthew 5:45

Jesus said, *"So likewise you, when you shall have done all those things which are commanded you, say, We are unprofitable servants: we have done that which was our duty to do."* Matthew 17:10

Jesus said, *"Peace be unto you: as My Father has sent Me, even so send I you."* John 20:21

"My dear child, your care and My love expressed to others pleases Me. My love is personal, yet impartial. You now understand and co-operate with it. It pleases Me when you take no credit for the work of My love. You now clearly see what My Spirit of love and healing can do. You also are pleased. Let us press on to further co-labor together, as I send you to new needs and new places."

May 27

"Therefore if any man be in Christ, he is a new creature: old things are passed away; behold, all things are become new." II Corinthians 5:17

"That you put off concerning the former conversation the old man, which is corrupt according to the deceitful lusts; And be renewed in the spirit of your mind; and that you put on the new man, which after God is created in righteousness and true holiness." Ephesians 4:22-24

"For I am the Lord, I change not." Malachi 3:6

"Your throne is established of old: You are from everlasting." Psalm 93:2

"Behold, I make all things new everyday. Even your very blood that nourishes every cell is renewed daily. It's a deception to imagine anything constant and consistently the same. Delight yourself in the new within you and without. I am the only unchanging one. I never fail."

May 28

"And suddenly there came a sound from heaven as of a rushing mighty wind, and it filled all the house where they were sitting." Acts 2:2

"I cried unto the Lord with my voice, and He heard me out of His holy hill." Psalm 3:4

"Our help is in the Name of the Lord, who made heaven and earth." Psalm 124:8

"And the tables were the work of God, and the writing was the writing of God, graven upon the tables." Exodus 32:16

"Behold the wind and the breezes, the air that surrounds you. This is how close I am. I hear every cry to Me. I send help in many forms. Only those who have eyes to see recognize Me in this, and are thankful. I send Heavenly and earthly messengers, servants, and help. My work is the origin of drama on earth. I write through many means."

May 29

"That I may know Him, and the power of His resurrection, and the fellowship of His sufferings, being made conformable unto His death." Philippians 3:10

"Look upon mine affliction and my pain; and forgive all my sins." Psalm 25:18

Jesus, "Who His own self bare our sins in His own body on the tree, that we, being dead to sins, should live unto righteousness: by whose stripes you were healed." 1 Peter 2:24

Jesus said, "And I will pray the Father, and He shall send you another Comforter, that He may abide with you forever." John 14:16

"What is the fellowship of My sufferings? You cannot avoid suffering. There is much pain as you face your own unrighteousness and sins. There is much pain from the sins of others and outer circumstances. But, you can bear them with Me, as I know all, and give whatever you need to press on close to Me. I love you as a Friend who knows and responds rightly to everything about you. This is the great comfort of My Spirit that never fails."

May 30

"Let nothing be done through strife or vainglory; but in lowliness of mind let each esteem other better than themselves. Look not every man on his own things, but every man also on the things of others." Philippians 2:3-4

"Bless them which persecute you: bless, and curse not. Rejoice with them that do rejoice, and weep with them that weep. Be of the same mind one toward another. Mind not high things, but condescend to men of low estate. Be not wise in your own conceits." Romans 12:14-16

Jesus said, "Take heed, and beware of covetousness: for a man's life consists not in the abundance of the things which he possesses." Luke 12:15

"For our heart shall rejoice in Him, because we have trusted in His holy Name." Psalm 33:21

"Doing others good is a life long learning. Giving your best, learning to put others first, is My way to a joyful life. I don't hold anything good back from those who walk uprightly. Yes, hold all things loosely, and bless where you can. I love the sound of a free heart, flowing in joy, laughter, praise song, and generosity."

May 31

Jesus said, "Write the things which you have seen, and the things which are, and the things which shall be hereafter."
Revelation 1:19

"So shall My Word be that goes forth out of My mouth: it shall not return unto Me void, but it shall accomplish that which I please, and it shall prosper in the thing whereto I sent it." Isaiah 55:11

Jesus said, "It is written, Man shall not live by bread alone, but by every Word that proceeds out of the mouth of God."
Matthew 4:4

"Let the words of my mouth, and the meditation of my heart, be acceptable in Your sight, O Lord, my strength, and my Redeemer." Psalm 19:14

"To write is an inspiration from Me. It allows you to focus on words. Meditate and share them. I speak, and My Words create and bring life and transformation. Your words can do likewise, when inspired by Me. I use many means to communicate My Word, My love, and My comfort."

June

June 1

"For Your lovingkindness is before my eyes: and I have walked in Your truth." Psalm 26:3

"Give her the fruit of her hands; and let her own works praise her in the gates." Proverbs 31:31

"The fruit of the righteous is a tree of life; and he that wins souls is wise." Proverbs 11:30

"I am the vine, you are the branches: He that abides in Me, and I in him, the same brings forth much fruit: for without Me you can do nothing." John 15:5

"You can rest in the certainty that you are walking your journey with Me, when you enjoy all the everyday events and details with Me. Then, just your presence, words, and deeds influence others towards Me. We accomplish fruit together; you drawing from My wine stock continually. Who could ask for more?"

June 2

"The God of my rock; in Him will I trust: He is my shield, and the horn of my salvation, my high tower, and my refuge, my Saviour; You save me from violence." II Samuel 22:3

"For to one is given by the Spirit the word of wisdom; to another the word of knowledge by the same Spirit; To another faith by the same Spirit; to another the gifts of healing by the same Spirit." 1 Corinthians 12:8-9

"But my God shall supply all your need according to His riches in glory by Christ Jesus." Philippians 4:19

"Oh that men would praise the Lord for His goodness, and for His wonderful works to the children of men!" Psalm 107:21

"Trust, trust, trust Me. Continue to ask for My gift of faith and wisdom. Everyday presents new needs within you and outside, around you. I am sufficient for everything needed. It's My delight to bless, surprise, and provide for My children."

June 3

"For You, Lord, will bless the righteous; with favor will You compass him as with a shield." Psalm 5:12

"I exhort therefore, that, first of all, supplications, prayers, intercessions, and giving of thanks, be made for all men; For kings, and for all that are in authority; that we may lead a quiet and peaceable life in all Godliness and honesty." 1 Timothy 2:1-2

"He that follows after righteousness and mercy finds life, righteousness, and honour." Proverbs 21:21

"Oh how great is Your goodness, which You have laid up for them that fear You; which You have wrought for them that trust in You before the sons of men!" Psalm 31:19

"Be right with Me, yourself, and others. This brings My peace that enables your heart to rest and be glad in Me. Therefore, you become My channel to all life around. Even the animals and plants respond to My Spirit of peace. Realize how valued you are by Me, and how much good I shower on you."

June 4

"For He knows our frame; He remembers that we are dust." Psalm 103:14

Jesus said, "The spirit truly is ready, but the flesh is weak." Mark 14:38

"By humility and the fear of the Lord are riches, and honour, and life." Proverbs 22:4

"He gives power to the faint; and to them that have no might He increases strength." Isaiah 40:29

"Your recognition of your frail humanity and your ability to do nothing without Me, is a sign of progress. Moving forward means deeper surrender to your place as My child with a mighty Father. In your humility, I infuse you with courage and My power to exercise your will rightly."

June 5

Jesus said, "Come unto Me, all you that labor and are heavy laden, and I will give you rest.
Take My yoke upon you, and learn of Me; for I am meek and lowly in heart: and you shall find rest unto your souls.
For My yoke is easy, and My burden is light." Matthew 11:28-30

"Rest in the Lord, and wait patiently for Him: fret not yourself because of him who prospers in his way, because of the man who brings wicked devices to pass." Psalm 37:7

Jesus said, "Take therefore no thought for the morrow: for the morrow shall take thought for the things of itself.
Sufficient unto the day is the evil thereof." Matthew 6:34

"And My people shall dwell in a peaceable habitation, and in sure dwellings, and in quiet resting places." Isaiah 32:18

"Rest. Take My yoke which is easy and light. Rest a season, and return to labor with only what I require. Don't fret over things not done. Hold fast to me for today's labor, and leave tomorrow's to wait. Rest, I say, take My rest."

June 6

"A friend loves at all times, and a brother is born for adversity." Proverbs 17:17

"Let us therefore come boldly unto the throne of grace, that we may obtain mercy, and find grace to help in time of need." Hebrews 4:16

Jesus said, "Ask, and it shall be given you; seek, and you shall find; knock and it shall be opened unto you." Matthew 7:7

"Rejoice evermore." 1 Thessalonians 5:17

"Yes, I am the friend to sinners. All men need Me in some capacity. Would that all would seek and find Me. Rejoice that you have many years in My leadership and companionship."

June 7

Jesus said, "This is My commandment, that you love one another, as I have loved you." John 15:12

"And above all things have fervent charity among yourselves: for charity shall cover the multitude of sins." 1 Peter 4:8

"You will show me the path of life: in Your presence is fulness of joy; at Your right hand there are pleasures forevermore." Psalm 16:11

Charity "Rejoices not in iniquity, but rejoices in the truth; Bears all things, believes all things, hopes all things, endures all things. Charity never fails." 1 Corinthians 13:6-8

"Yes, I have commanded that you love one another. This is only consistently possible with My help and wisdom as your choice. My love paves the highest path of life on earth. Recognize My image in even the lowest of humanity. Therein lies the greatest potential for good."

June 8

"But You, O Lord, shall endure forever; and Your remembrance unto all generations." Psalm 102:12

"You are of God, little children, and have overcome them: because greater is He that is in you, than he that is in the world." 1 John 4:4

"I have rejoiced in the way of Your testimonies, as much as in all riches." Psalm 119:14

"For we are the circumcision, which worship God in the Spirit, and rejoice in Christ Jesus, and have no confidence in the flesh." Philippians 3:3

"Haven't I shown Myself as ever present, ever loving, ever aware of true needs, training My people to overcome themselves, the world, and their enemies? Therefore, rejoice in your life journey with Me. Enjoy, laugh, love, and bring all this to others. Have no anxiety, as I lead you moment by moment."

June 9

"And he showed me a pure river of water of life, clear as crystal, proceeding out of the throne of God and of the Lamb." Revelation 22:1

"Let us lay aside every weight, and the sin which does so easily beset us, and let us run with patience the race that is set before us." Hebrews 12:1

Live in the wonder of who I Am and all that you see flowing from My river of life and goodness. Yes, your life on earth has many obstacles and challenges, but I came to overcome them all. So, keep on learning, running, and surrendering to My will."

June 10

"Why so downcast O my soul...?" Psalm 42:5a

"Rejoice evermore. Pray without ceasing. In everything give thanks: for this is the will of God in Christ Jesus concerning you. 1 Thessalonians 5:16-18

"Rejoice in the Lord always: and again I say rejoice." Philippians 4:4

"Don't let your soul be downcast on gray and ordinary days of labor and details. Rejoice in another day on earth, to think on Me, to see My handiwork all around you, and to rejoice as I answer your prayers."

June 11

"Enter into His gates with thanksgiving, and into His courts with praise: be thankful unto Him...." Psalm 100:4

"Let this mind be in you, which was also in Christ Jesus." Philippians 2:5

"I receive your praise and thanksgiving with the satisfaction of a Father, knowing all is well with My child. Enjoy that childlike place of security and peace. Let My mind be in you as you live and observe the world."

June 12

"I have made the earth, and created man upon it: I, even My hands, have stretched out the heavens, and all their hosts have I commanded." Isaiah 45:12

"Through faith we understand that the worlds were framed by the Word of God, so that things which are seen were not made of things which do appear." Hebrews 11:3

"From whence come wars and fightings among you?" James 4:1a

"Yes, it is My Word and My hand that holds the world together, that keeps it turning in order. O, that the people of the world would know Me in this way and lay aside their blind selfishness, greed, and harm to one another and find there is My sufficiency and salvation for all."

June 13

"Let not your heart be troubled, neither let it be afraid" John 14:27

"Keep your heart with all diligence: for out of it are the issues of life." Proverbs 4:23

"Your Word is a lamp unto my feet, and a light unto my path." Psalm 119:105

"Do not allow fear to enter your heart. This will stop the flow of My Spirit. Keep looking to Me and guard your heart and mind by receiving My Words and thoughts. In these days, many are making decisions from fear. Continue to go your way, rejoicing in Me and see how I guide and protect you."

June 14

"There is a way which seems right to a man, but the end thereof are the ways of death." Proverbs 14:12

"For God is not the author of confusion, but of peace, as in all churches of the saints." 1 Corinthians 14:33

"There are many theories and ideas of man abounding in information. Don't be confused or overwhelmed. My simple command to love Me and love your neighbor as yourself holds true forever and is sufficient to stabilize you in all your life."

June 15

"Give unto the Lord the glory due unto His Name; worship the Lord in the beauty of holiness." Psalm 29:2

Jesus said, "I am come that they might have life, and that they might have it more abundantly." John 10:10

"But Godliness with contentment is great gain." 1 Timothy 6:6

"You ask for beauty. Holiness brings true beauty, a radiance of peace, content where I lead. All things that are needed for holiness, wholeness, I freely provide for those who love Me; love the Truth and follow My Way."

June 16

Jesus said, "And I will pray the Father, and He shall give you another Comforter, that He may abide with you forever; even the Holy Spirit of truth...." John 14:16-17

"Delight yourself also in the Lord; and He shall give you the desires of your heart." Psalm 37:4

"Allow Me to comfort you as a Father when His child is saddened and disappointed. Don't press your expectations hard on the world. In close companionship with Me, quietly wait as I fulfill your desires as I know what is best for you and others."

June 17

"Wherefore God also has highly exalted Him (Jesus) and given Him a Name which is above every name." Philippians 2:9

Jesus said, "I will never leave you, nor forsake you." Hebrews 13:5

"When you call My Name, I hear, I understand, I act. My Spirit attends you and helps you. Believe and trust I am with you."

June 18

"And in the morning, rising up a great while before day, He (Jesus) went out, and departed into a solitary place, and there prayed." Mark 1:35

"I exhort therefore, that, first of all, supplications, prayers, intercessions, and giving of thanks, be made for all men." 1 Timothy 2:1

"There are times when it seems that I have set you aside from my work. This is never the case. I give you seasons of quietness and solitude and restoring and less activity. I have many of My children in quiet, obscure, hidden places with Me. I treasure them in their humility and prayer for the world."

June 19

Jesus said, "Go into all the world, and preach the Gospel to every creature." Mark 16:15

Jesus said, "I send you forth as sheep in the midst of wolves: be therefore wise as serpents, and harmless as doves." Matthew 10:16

"Be not conformed to this world: but be transformed by the renewing of your mind, that you may prove what is that good, and acceptable, and perfect will of God." Romans 12:2

"Fear not, Abram: I am your shield, and your exceeding great reward." Genesis 15:1

"Fear not to go in My Name when I send you. You will experience the deepest joy and satisfaction as you see the transformation of others by My Love and My Word. I Am your protector, your shield, and your defender."

June 20

"Rejoice, because your names are written in Heaven." Luke 10:20

And there shall in no wise enter into it any thing that defiles, neither whatsoever works abomination, or makes a lie: but they which are written in the Lamb's book of life. Revelations 21:27

"And the Lord shall guide you continually, and satisfy your soul in drought, and make fat your bones: and you shall be like a watered garden, and like a spring of water, whose waters fail not." Isaiah 58:11

"Rejoice in knowing Me, that your name is written in My Book of Life. My glory and riches are available to My children. Let your heart be satisfied in this knowledge of Me. Sing in the garden of your heart."

June 21

What? Know ye not that your body is the temple of the Holy Ghost which is in you, which ye have of God, and ye are not your own? 1 Corinthians 6:19

The Lord bless thee, and keep thee: The Lord make his face shine upon thee, and be gracious unto thee: The Lord lift up his countenance upon thee, and give thee peace. Numbers 6:24-26

Thou wilt keep him in perfect peace, whose mind is stayed on Thee: because he trusteth in Thee. Isaiah 26:3

"Dear child, your life is not your own. Remember, you've given your life over to My will and purposes. I call you to the hurting. lonely, and lost. Do not be overwhelmed or overburdened by sadness and pity. Neither you, nor I, am helpless to engage and rescue and heal. Continue to reach them, even in quiet, silent gestures and prayer. My healing, calling power goes out through you, and I will prevail."

June 22

"Now faith is the substance of things hoped for, the evidence of things not seen." Hebrews 11:1

"Let this mind be in you, which was also in Christ Jesus." Philippians 2:5

"To see others as I see them, and to treat them as if they were whom I desire them to be is a gift of My Mind imparted to those who know and love Me well."

June 23

"In everything give thanks: for this is the will of God in Christ Jesus concerning you." 1 Thessalonians 5:18

"The goodness of God leads you to repentance." Romans 2:4

"Let everyday find you more united in love with and thankful to Me. I Am your Father, your Creator, and it's My pleasure to give you gifts. The gift of repentance frees you to be thankful and loving more. So imitate Me in your daily life—forgive, give, and love as I love you."

June 24

"Jesus said, "Suffer the little children to come unto Me, and forbid them not: for of such is the Kingdom of God. Verily I say unto you, Whosoever shall not receive the Kingdom of God as a little child, he shall not enter therein." Mark 10:14-15

Jesus said, "Verily I say unto you, except you be converted, and become as little children, you shall not enter into the Kingdom of Heaven. Whosoever therefore shall humble himself as this little child, the same is greatest in the Kingdom of Heaven. And whoso shall receive one such little child in My Name receives Me." Matthew 18:3-5

"Bring the little children to Me, as you cause them to know, enjoy, and recognize My Spirit in you. This makes a sweet, comforting impression that will not be forgotten nor unfruitful."

June 25

Jesus is the "friend that sticks closer than a brother." Proverbs 18:24

Jesus said, "I have called you friends, for all things that I have heard of My Father I have made known unto you." John 15:15

"Weeping may endure for a night, but joy comes in the morning." Psalm 30:5

"Be of good cheer My child. I am your close companion in the grey and weary days. See if I will not brighten and strengthen you to rejoice in this day."

June 26

"Hear counsel, and receive instruction, that you may be wise in your latter end. There are many devices in a man's heart; nevertheless the counsel of the Lord, that shall stand." Proverbs 19:20-21

Jesus said, "I am the vine, you are the branches: he that abides in Me, and I in him, the same brings forth much fruit: for without Me you can do nothing." John 15:5

"Wait on the Lord: be of good courage, and He shall strengthen thine heart: wait, I say, on the Lord." Psalm 27:14

"Wait upon Me, My child. You can make nothing happen ahead of My timing. I hear your heart prayers and the prayers of those whose release you long for. Trust that I know what's best."

June 27

"I press toward the mark for the prize of the high calling of God in Christ Jesus." Philippians 3:14

Jesus said, "If the world hates you, you know that it hated Me before it hated you. If you were of the world, the world would love his own: but because you are not of the world, but I have chosen you out of the world, therefore the world hates you." John 15:18-19

"And now abides faith, hope, charity, these three; but the greatest of these is charity." 1 Corinthians 13:13

"Press on, My child. Keep the hope before you that I carry you through all the pain and misunderstanding from the world. Yes, faith stays strong, love is poured out, and hope knows success and fulfillment."

June 28

"But You are holy, You that inhabit the praises of Israel." Psalm 22:3

"How sweet are Your Words to my taste! Yes sweeter than honey to my mouth." Psalm 119:103

"...no good thing will He withhold from them that walk uprightly." Psalm 84:11

"Your adoration, praise, and prayers make a sweet atmosphere for others and draw Me close. You have been told you don't deserve good things, that you must accept whatever others send your way, that this is who you are. No, look to My Words, child, and rejoice as you are My precious, enriched one. The confusion and hurt are healed by My embrace and anointing for life."

June 29

"That the God of our Lord Jesus Christ, the Father of glory, may give unto you the Spirit of wisdom and revelation in the knowledge of Him." Ephesians 1:17

"...there is a God in Heaven that reveals secrets." Daniel 2:28

"...as the Bridegroom rejoices over the bride, so shall your God rejoice over you." Isaiah 62:5

"I am revealing many things to you as I prepare My Bride to meet Me. Have no fear for the future. I am coming for My Bride, and nothing can hinder My coming nor My Bride's preparation. You are veiled, covered unto Me. Let not your heart be troubled. Take My yoke, take My peace."

June 30

"Give and it shall be given unto you; good measure, pressed down, and shaken together, and running over, shall men give into your bosom. For with the same measure that you [give out] it shall be measured to you again." Luke 6:38

Jesus said, "It is more blessed to give than to receive." Acts 20:35

"...there is no God else beside Me; a just God and a Saviour; there is none beside Me." Isaiah 45:21

"Give and it shall be given to you with good measure. I am just, and the "Great Equalizer." This is not man's work. Only I know the needs and hearts of man. Your part is to be a generous giver as I lead."

July

July 1

"So God created man in His own image, in the image of God created He him; male and female created He them."
Genesis 1:27

"...that He would grant you, according to the riches of His glory, to be strengthened with might by His Spirit in the inner man." Ephesians 3:16

"And to know the love of Christ, which passes knowledge, that you might be filled with all the fullness of God." Ephesians 3:19

"I have made you in My image with the capacity to think and feel as I do. That capacity grows in fullness according to your choice to know and follow Me. When you choose Me, you choose abundant life with My peace and joy. These are the true riches."

July 2

Jesus said, "In the world you shall have tribulation: but be of good cheer; I have overcome the world." John 16:33

"It is of the Lord's mercies that we are not consumed, because His compassions fail not. They are new every morning: great is your faithfulness." Lamentations 3:22-23

Jesus said, "Judge not according to the appearance, but judge righteous judgment." John 7:24

"The sun will shine again and you'll forget these gray, wet days. But remember My faithfulness through all days. Be of good cheer. Let all criticism fall away, and be glad for all life before you."

July 3

"For the gifts and calling of God are without repentance." Romans 11:29

"...mercy rejoices against judgment." James 2:13

"And above all things have fervent charity among yourselves: for charity shall cover the multitude of sins." 1 Peter 4:8

"I've called you out to care for, in mercy, My people. Keep your eyes on the immediate before you. Reinforce, draw out, the qualities of Me that you see in others. Demonstrate My character openly. Take courage from Me. Don't be intimidated."

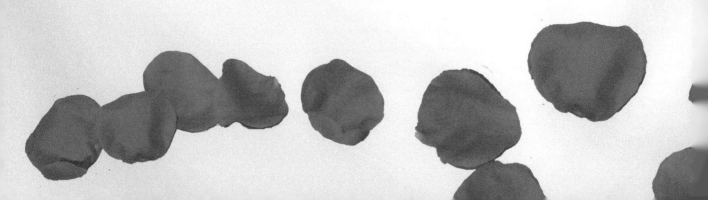

July 4

"Even so then at this present time also there is a remnant according to the election of grace. Romans 11:5

"Have salt in yourselves, and have peace one with another." Mark 9:50

"You are the salt of the earth." Matthew 5:13

"Wherefore we, receiving a Kingdom which cannot be moved, let us serve God acceptably with reverence and Godly fear." Hebrews 12:28

"Know that I have a remnant in this land who have not, and will not bow their knee to other gods. They are the salt that preserves and they will be at the forefront of answers and hope when My new Kingdom order comes. I have a plan. The government is on My shoulders."

July 5

"…the power of the Lord was present to heal them." Luke 5:17

"And when He had called unto Him His twelve disciples, He gave them power against unclean spirits, to cast them out, and to heal all manner of sickness and all manner of disease." Matthew 10:1

"According as His divine power has given unto us all things that pertain unto life and Godliness, through the knowledge of Him that has called us to glory and virtue." II Peter 1:3

"I am your healer. Co-operate with Me in simplicity, cleanliness, order, and peace. I've created all you need for life and Godliness."

July 6

"For the earth shall be filled with the knowledge of the glory of the Lord, as the waters cover the sea." Habakkuk 2:14

"To everything there is a season, and a time for every purpose under the heaven." Ecclesiastes 3:1

Wherefore gird up the loins of your mind, be sober, and hope to the end for the grace that is to be brought unto you at the revelation of Jesus Christ." 1 Peter 1:13

"There is a time when all men must ask for the meaning and purpose of their lives. I await that time when I can show them My reality. I am the Creator God who intends a purpose for all I create. Nothing but knowing Me will fully answer this question for each individual person."

July 7

"That He would grant you according to the riches of His glory, to be strengthened with might by His Spirit in the inner man." Ephesians 3:16

"You therefore endure hardness as a good soldier of Jesus Christ." II Timothy 2:3

"...for he that comes to God must believe that He is, and that He is a rewarder of them who diligently seek Him." Hebrews 11:6

"These are days of inner renewal and strengthening. This is accomplishment enough. Let the world go by in its mad race for empty goals. I will have a prepared army to lead My cause in these days. Cultivate your inner garden with Me. I reward, in ways the world cannot know, those who diligently seek Me; those whose joy and success is in Me."

July 8

"But my God shall supply all your need according to His riches in glory by Christ Jesus." Philippians 4:19

"That if you shall confess with your mouth the Lord Jesus, and shall believe in your heart that God has raised Him from the dead, you shall be saved." Romans 10:9

"You see around you My abundant provision. Enjoy and give out of My abundance. Have no worry for the future and how I will care for your loved ones. They are in My hands as you have asked. Let Me direct your thoughts, expectations, and love poured out."

July 9

"But there is a God in Heaven that reveals secrets." Daniel 2:28

"He reveals the deep and secret things, He knows what is in the darkness, and the light dwells with Him." Daniel 2:22

"For in much wisdom is much grief: and he that increases knowledge increases sorrow." Ecclesiastes 1:18

"But rejoice, inasmuch as you are partakers of Christ's sufferings; that, when His glory shall be revealed, you may be glad also with exceeding joy." 1 Peter 4:13

"I reveal the secret things to My friends. Be glad in this, even when you know there is much sorrow in much wisdom. I would have ones to bear My sorrows with Me. There is a loneliness in your closeness to Me that no man can fill."

July 10

"That in the dispensation of the fullness of times He might gather together in one all things in Christ, both which are in heaven and which are on earth; even in Him." Ephesians 1:10

"...for at the time of the end shall be the vision." Daniel 8:17

"And beside this, giving all diligence, add to your faith virtue; and to virtue knowledge; and to knowledge temperance; and to temperance patience; and to patience Godliness; and to Godliness brotherly kindness; and to brotherly kindness charity." II Peter 1:5-7

"I have set before you an open door, and no man can shut it." Revelation 3:8

"Hold fast the visions I am giving you—to be fulfilled in the fullness of time. Patiently persevere in My service. I will open the way, give you favor, and establish you."

July 11

"Cease from anger, and forsake wrath: fret not yourself in any wise to do evil." Psalm 37:8

"And you shall love the Lord your God with all your heart, and with all your soul, and with all your mind, and with all your strength: this is the first commandment. And the second is like, namely this, you shall love your neighbor as yourself. There is none other commandment greater than these." Mark 12:30-31

"And we know that all things work together for good to them that love God, to them who are the called according to His purpose." Romans 8:28

"My child, do not fret over matters and details of little importance. Walk gently with Me, loving yourself and others with mercy, not judgment. Remember My tender, protective, providing love; My working all for good, and do likewise."

July 12

*"I will lift up my eyes unto the hills, from whence comes my help. My help comes from the Lord,
which made heaven and earth." Psalm 121:1-2*

*"My son, despise not the chastening of the Lord; neither be weary of His correction: For whom the Lord loves
He corrects; even as a father the son in whom he delights." Proverbs 3:11-12*

"Reprove one that has understanding and he will understand knowledge." Proverbs 19:25

"Yes, your help comes from the hills, from looking up to Me. One day all the daily concerns and small matters of your life will have no more influence on you. Indeed, you will know and wonder why you allowed them to assume more importance than necessary. It's My training time and training requires repetition, reflection, and correction to develop right habits."

July 13

Jesus said, "He has sent Me to bind up the brokenhearted." Luke 4:18

The church is cleansed "with the washing of water by the Word." Ephesians 5:26

"I will say of the Lord, He is my refuge and my fortress: my God; in Him will I trust." Psalm 91:2

"You are the salt of the earth." Matthew 5:13 "You are the light of the world." Matthew 5:14

"Yes, I am close and available to the brokenhearted. As you walk close to Me, you will be strengthened to be both salt and light to the sufferings and questions of others. Be not afraid to embrace the hurting, as I lead. There will be no contamination, absorption, or projection against you. I am there, living through you, doing what I need to do. My Word cleanses you.

July 14

"They shall bring forth fruit in old age." Psalm 92:14

"In the beginning God created the heaven and the earth." Genesis 1:1

"...times of refreshing shall come from the presence of the Lord." Acts 3:19

"You will find no aging, no deterioration in Me, just ever expanding love. Catching up the universe and sending it out anew, this is my joy, my delight. Think on this in relation to your small concerns and find the rest and refreshing I have for you."

July 15

"But unto you that fear My Name shall the Sun of righteousness arise with healing in His wings; and you shall go forth, and grow up as calves of the stall." Malachi 4:2

"He has filled the hungry with good things." Luke 1:53

"The grace of the Lord Jesus Christ, and the love of God, and the communion of the Holy Spirit, be with you all. Amen." II Corinthians 13:14

"I move My children to ever new seasons of growth and maturity. There is a constant unfolding of truth revealed to those who will receive. Be a good receiver, humble and hungry to know more and ever more of Me. I delight in this communion and relationship."

July 16

"As for God, His way is perfect: the way of the Lord is tried: He is a buckler to all those who trust in Him."
Psalm 18:30

"Great and marvelous are your works, Lord God Almighty; just and true are your ways." Revelation 15:3

"But the God of all grace, who has called us unto His eternal glory by Christ Jesus, after you have suffered a while, make you perfect, stablish, strengthen, settle you." 1 Peter 5:10

"Yes, My child, My way is perfect. As you survey your life, you can understand My perfect justice in allowing suffering and environments that encourage you to know yourself and desire to know Me. I always seek your highest good in ways only your contact with Me can show to be necessary and meaningful."

July 17

"A wise man will hear, and will increase learning; and a man of understanding shall attain unto wise counsels."
Proverbs 1:5

"Keep your heart with all diligence; for out of it are the issues of life." Proverbs 4:23

"But exhort one another daily while it is called today; lest any of you be hardened through the deceitfulness of sin."
Hebrews 3:13

"Yes, I want you to be always learning, always open to new revelation. Guard your heart. Stay tender, compassionate, and above all do not judge. My Spirit will always show My mind. Avoid hard, closed opinions and that which does not bring My life of faith, hope, and charity in abundance."

July 18

"This know also, that in the last days perilous times shall come. For men shall be lovers of their own selves."
II Timothy 3:1-2

"The Lord is my strength and my shield; my heart trusts in Him, and I am helped: therefore my heart greatly rejoices; and with my song will I praise Him." Psalm 28:7

"Now the God of patience and consolation grant you to be like-minded one toward another according to Christ Jesus."
Romans 15:5

"Dependency on Me brings you a freedom and joy that man desires and searches for in many other ways. My way brings a rich and fruitful life, but self-will brings sin and eventual death. It grieves Me when My children choose their own way without My guidance and help. But, I am a patient and forgiving God."

July 19

"…you shall rejoice in all that you put your hand unto, you and your household: wherein the Lord your God has blessed you." Deuteronomy 12:7

"Who shall tell you words, whereby you and all your house shall be saved." Acts 11:14

"And God blessed them, and God said unto them, Be fruitful and multiply, and replenish the earth." Genesis 1:28

"When my father and my mother forsake me, then the Lord will take me up." Psalm 27:10

"Family, family, family. I created family. I said be fruitful and multiply. I desire a heritage. I want My people to bloom and bear fruit and seed. I pour My Spirit and life through you to strengthen the ties of family and friends. Give life and draw life from Me and one another."

July 20

"Trust in the Lord with all your heart; and lean not unto your own understanding. In all your ways acknowledge Him, and He shall direct your paths." Proverbs 3:5-6

Jesus said, "For the Son of man is come to seek and to save that which was lost." Luke 19:10

"...do I seek to please men? For if I yet pleased men, I should not be the servant of Christ." Galatians 1:10

"Lean on Me, not on the opinions of man. Be strong in knowledge of Me as well as your weakness. Humble dependence and simplicity keep My Gospel alive and attractive to those who are lost. I am always searching for the lost."

July 21

"For this purpose the Son of God was manifested, that He might destroy the works of the devil."
1 John 3:8

God said, "I have spoken it, I will also bring it to pass; I have purposed it, I will also do it."
Isaiah 46:11

"But exhort one another daily, while it is called today; lest any of you be hardened through the deceitfulness of sin." Hebrews 3:13

"Now the Lord of peace Himself give you peace always by all means." II Thessalonians 3:16

"I am a God of purpose and continuous creativity. For each life there is My good purpose. Encourage and exhort others in My good purpose in every season. My peace I leave with you."

July 22

"Forgetting those things which are behind, and reaching forth unto those things which are before, I press toward the mark for the prize of the high calling of God in Christ Jesus." Philippians 3:13-14

"I the Lord am your Saviour and your Redeemer, the mighty One of Jacob." Isaiah 49:26

"Humble yourselves therefore under the mighty hand of God, that He may exalt you in due time: Casting all your care upon Him; for He cares for you." 1 Peter 5:6-7

Jesus said, "Take My yoke upon you and learn of Me." Matthew 11:29

"Learn from those times you regret, but go forward with renewed faith. I have redeemed and forgiven you. Take no care for past or future. Live now in My great, loving care, the care of your true Father."

July 23

"Your Kingdom is an everlasting Kingdom. and Your dominion endures throughout all generations." Psalm 145:13

"Your Word is a lamp unto my feet, and a light unto my path." Psalm 119:105

"Lord, You have been our dwelling place in all generations." Psalm 90:1

"For the law was given by Moses, but grace and truth came by Jesus Christ." John 1:17

"Establish My dominion, My Kingdom, as your dwelling place. Keep Me and My Word central and you will experience unshakable balance as you walk through the world. I am your unshakable center point, always bringing you back to my truth."

July 24

Jesus said, "I came not to call the righteous, but sinners to repentance." Mark 2:17

"For Godly sorrow works repentance to salvation not to be repented of: but the sorrow of the world works death."
II Corinthians 7:10

The Lord Jesus "is long suffering toward us, not willing that any should perish, but that all should come to repentance."
II Peter 3:9

"If we confess our sins, He is faithful and just to forgive us our sins, and to cleanse us from all unrighteousness." 1 John 1:9

"True repentance comes from a heart of remorse for the damage and hurt done to others and oneself. There is a resolve to turn from the sinful, evil doings, and an honest confession of the motive behind the sin."

July 25

"The Lord is far from the wicked: but He hears the prayer of the righteous." Proverbs 15:29

"But we will give ourselves continually to prayer, and to the ministry of the Word." Acts 6:4

"Let us therefore come boldly unto the throne of grace, that we may obtain mercy, and find grace to help in time of need." Hebrews 4:16

"Confess your faults one to another, and pray one for another, that you may be healed. The effectual fervent prayer of a righteous man avails much." James 4:16

"My answer to prayer is to send help in the form most needed, at the time, to do the greatest good to the greatest number of people. Often this goes unrecognized. My love is freely given out in many ways and forms. Only those whose hearts are in touch with mine can truly begin to grasp the extent of My love."

July 26

Jesus said, "My sheep hear My voice, and I know them, and they follow Me." John 10:27

We "desire that you might be filled with the knowledge of His will in all wisdom and spiritual understanding; that you might walk worthy of the Lord unto all pleasing, being fruitful in every good work, and increasing in the knowledge of God." Colossians 1:9-10

"For I will pour water upon him that is thirsty, and floods upon the dry ground: I will pour My Spirit upon your seed, and My blessing upon your offspring." Isaiah 44:3

Jesus said, "...freely you have received, freely give." Matthew 10:8

"Yes, as you choose to follow My guidance in all of your life, you will live the best, the richest, and the most fruitful life possible on earth. This is My love poured continually on those who know Me through My Son Jesus. Receive and be glad in My abundance. Give willingly of My abundant life—joy, laughter, provision."

July 27

Jesus said, "If any man thirst, let him come unto Me and drink. He that believes on Me, as the Scripture has said, out of his belly shall flow rivers of Living Water." John 7:38

"I made myself servant unto all, that I might gain the more." 1 Corinthians 9:19

"...to every purpose there is time and judgment." Ecclesiastes 8:6

Jesus said, "Blessed are they which do hunger and thirst after righteousness: for they shall be filled." Matthew 5:6

"Don't berate yourself for not doing more for others. Your being with them, doing the small things you can do have more quiet power from Me than you can see. As always, the purpose and results are Mine."

July 28

Jesus said, "I will pray the Father, and He shall give you another Comforter, that He may abide with you forever." John 14:16

Jesus said, "Blessed are they that mourn: for they shall be comforted." Matthew 5:4

Jesus said, "When you pray, say, Our Father which art in Heaven, Hallowed be your Name." Luke 11:2

"Now then we are ambassadors for Christ." II Corinthians 5:20

"I am the great Comforter. I desire to comfort every loss, grief, and pain. Only those who call Me Father can experience My comfort. So, be My ambassadors of comfort and reveal My love to those who do not know it yet."

July 29

It is of the Lord's mercies that we are not consumed, because His compassions fail not. They are new every morning: great is Your faithfulness." Lamentations 3:22-23

"Rejoice in the Lord always: and again I say rejoice." Philippians 4:4

Jesus said, "Arise go your way: your faith has made you whole." Luke 17:19

"Surely goodness and mercy shall follow me all the days of my life: and I will dwell in the house of the Lord forever." Psalm 23:6

"I am the God of the new-every-morning mercies and goodness. Receive what you need and go your way rejoicing. There is deep rest and replenishment only I can give. It's My desire to see My children well and whole."

July 30

"O Lord, how manifold are Your works! In wisdom have You made them all: the earth is full of Your riches."
Psalm 104:24

God said, "For every beast of the forest is Mine, and the cattle upon a thousand hills." Psalm 50:10

"Let them shout for joy, and be glad that favor My righteous cause: yes, let them say continually, Let the Lord be magnified, which has pleasure in the prosperity of His servant." Psalm 35:27

"But My God shall supply all your need according to His riches in glory by Christ Jesus." Philippians 4:19

"I am your Provider. I own all the wealth of earth. As I direct, be generous. I see all needs. I hear the prayers and order help and comfort and supply. I use My servants in many unseen and unknown ways."

July 31

"When you lie down, you shall not be afraid: yes, you shall lie down, and your sleep shall be sweet." Proverbs 3:24

"Many, O Lord my God, are Your wonderful works which You have done, and Your thoughts which are to us: they cannot be reckoned up in order to You: if I would declare and speak of them, they are more than can be numbered."
Psalm 40:5

"And the very God of peace sanctify you wholly; and I pray God your whole spirit and soul and body be preserved blameless unto the coming of our Lord Jesus Christ." 1 Thessalonians 5:23

"For My thoughts are not your thoughts, neither are your ways My ways, says the Lord. For as the heavens are higher than the earth, so are My ways higher than your ways, and My thoughts than your thoughts." Isaiah 55:8-9

"Yes, I give My beloved children sweet sleep. Therein, I re-arrange, order, and cleanse body, soul, and spirit. Truly, My Father's heart is with and for you. This is the medicine that heals, uplifts, and forges new beginnings. Seek My answers to all your needs and questions. My vision and solutions are truer and higher than man's."

August

August 1

Jesus said, "I am the way, the truth, and the life: no man comes unto the Father, but by Me." John 14:6

"You have in love to my soul delivered it from the pit of corruption: for You have cast all my sins behind my back." Isaiah 38:16

"You will show me the path of life: in Your presence is fullness of joy; at Your right hand there are pleasures forevermore." Psalm 16:11

Jesus said, "Truly, truly, I say unto you, Except a man be born again, he cannot see the Kingdom of God." John 3:3

"I am the true, only way to real life: full, rich, meaningful life. Only those who cast themselves upon Me in abandoned love can begin to experience My powerful, loving care. My Kingdom is real, eternal, and open to whosoever will come to Me. I set the captives free."

August 2

Jesus said, "The harvest is plentiful, but the laborers are few; Pray you therefore the Lord of the harvest, that He would send forth laborers into His harvest." Matthew 9:37-38

Jesus said, "Abide in Me, and I in you. As the branch cannot bear fruit of itself, except it abide in the vine; no more can you, except you abide in Me." John 15:4

Jesus said, "I am the light of the world: he that follows Me shall not walk in darkness, but shall have the light of life." John 8:12

Jesus said, concerning the enemy of man, "The thief comes not, but for to steal, and to kill, and to destroy: I am come that they might have life, and that they might have it more abundantly." John 10:10

"I am the Lord of the harvest. I desire, and am preparing for, a great world harvest. My laborers have been, and are, long in the making. Rejoice in this work, and do not become weary. Draw on Me as the vine, your source of all that's needed to flourish. Look on the Light, not on the earth's darkness. Fear not. Be of good courage. Much of the enemy's tactic is to pollute the air with fearful, wrong thoughts and confusion. Live above all this in your spirit with My thoughts and peace. I am your good, loving Father."

August 3

"Submitting yourselves one to another in the fear of God." Ephesians 5:21

"Neither yield you your members as instruments of unrighteousness unto sin: but yield yourselves unto God." Romans 6:13

"Now no chastening for the present seems to be joyous, but grievous: nevertheless afterward it yields the peaceable fruit of righteousness unto them which are exercised thereby." Hebrews 12:11

"Dearly beloved, avenge not yourselves, but rather give place unto wrath: for it is written, Vengeance is mine; I will repay, says the Lord." Romans 12:19

"Submission is the way of the cross. Yielding to Me, to My truth and to others as I direct, brings the peaceable fruit of righteousness. There's wisdom in taking no offense and giving no retaliation on others in right human relationships."

August 4

"Wait on the Lord: be of good courage, and He shall strengthen your heart: wait, I say, on the Lord." Psalm 27:14

"The Lord is good unto them that wait for Him, to the soul that seeks Him." Lamentations 3:25

"See then that you walk circumspectly, not as fools, but as wise, redeeming the time, because the days are evil." Ephesians 5:15-16

"For I know the thoughts that I think toward you, says the Lord, thoughts of peace, and not of evil, to give you an expected end." Jeremiah 29:11

"Waiting upon Me is not time lost, but time set to good use, seeing Me in all those people and events that surround you. Learning of My ways and growing in wisdom is your best use of time. When you are ready to move to new seasons of experience, I know better than you, and release you to them. So wait in expectancy, learning by revelation of Me."

August 5

"And Jesus said unto him, I will come and heal him." Matthew 8:7

"And it shall come to pass, that whosoever shall call on the Name of the Lord shall be saved." Acts 2:21

"...to another the gifts of healing by the same Spirit." 1 Corinthians 12:9

"Behold, to obey is better than sacrifice." 1 Samuel 15:22

"Yes, all healing is from My hand, My Spirit, and My Word. All that is needed I make available to whomever calls upon Me in need. I use those gifted in healing to bring My healing and renewal in many ways. Often it is the spirit and soul of people that requires healing before the body will follow in line and balance. It grieves My Spirit when My truth and healing are not received nor applied to the pain of My children. Be one who hears and obeys My wisdom."

August 6

Jesus said, "But when you shall hear of wars and commotions, be not terrified: for these things must first come to pass; but the end is not by and by. Then said He unto them, Nation shall rise against nation, and Kingdom against Kingdom." Luke 21:9-10

"The Lord is my rock, and my fortress, and my deliverer; my God my strength, in whom I will trust." Psalm 18:2

"Of the increase of His government and peace, there shall be no end." Isaiah 9:7

Jesus said, "Take heed, and beware of covetousness: for a man's life consists not in the abundance of things which he possesses." Luke 12:15

"In the days ahead, there will be a great wave overtake the earth. Nations will be in uproar and not know what to do. They will be unable to establish the old order. Those who turn to My government will not perish, but be positioned to invite many into My Kingdom. Therefore, hold loosely the things of earth, hold firmly to Me and My people. I would have you prepared."

August 7

Jesus said, "And whosoever will be chief among you, let him be your servant." Matthew 20:27

"He that dwells in the secret place of the Most High shall abide under the shadow of the Almighty." Psalm 91:1

"Can two walk together, except they be agreed?" Amos 3:3

"Casting all your care upon Him; for He cares for you." 1 Peter 5:7

"I've called and appointed you to leadership. Not as one who desired a position before men, but the leadership in the secret place with Me. As you agree with Me, you lead with Me. This is how My Kingdom comes and My will is done on earth, as I lead from Heaven. Go on quietly with Me and be assured that what we agree on will be granted. I carry the burden so you can walk in great peace and confidence, trusting in Me alone."

August 8

"Teach me in your way, O Lord, and lead me in a plain path, because of my enemies." Psalm 27:11

"If any of you lack wisdom, let him ask of God, that gives to all men liberally, and upbraids not; and it shall be given him." James 1:5

"He restores my soul: He leads me in the paths of righteousness for His Name sake." Psalm 23:3

"And now abides faith, hope, charity, these three; but the greatest of these is charity." 1 Corinthians 13:13

"My Spirit fills you and leads you in the way of simplicity, keeping your thoughts on the moment you are living. Therefore your life is rich in meaning and revelation of Me in all situations. I am your teacher, providing wisdom as you ask for it. Above all get wisdom and your love capacity and peaceful effectiveness will grow."

August 9

"Many are the afflictions of the righteous: but the Lord delivers him out of them all." Psalm 34:19

"Withhold not Your tender mercies from me, O Lord: let Your loving kindness and truth continually preserve me." Psalm 40:11

Jesus said, "For God so loved the world, that He gave His only begotten Son, that whosoever believes in Him shall not perish, but have everlasting life." John 3:16

Jesus said, "Come unto Me, all you that labor and are heavy laden, and I will give you rest." Matthew 11:28

"Yes, I have compassion for the sufferings of mankind. I also am the answer to the sufferings of mankind. I sent My Son to show the way out of the results of mankind's sins. I am a just God. I wait for mankind to come to Me as I have come to them."

August 10

"Go you therefore, and teach all nations, baptizing them in the Name of the Father, and of the Son, and of the Holy Ghost." Matthew 28:19

"There is therefore now no condemnation to them which are in Christ Jesus, who walk not after the flesh, but after the Spirit." Romans 8:1

"For a just man falls seven times, and rises up again." Proverbs 24:16

Jesus said, " Her sins which are many, are forgiven; for she loved much: but to whom little is forgiven, the same loves little." Luke 7:47

"Go in My Name, represent who I am wherever I send you. I don't condemn you in your moments of weakness and humanity. Don't condemn yourself. Rise up again in your spirit, recognize your need, return again and again to My forgiving, understanding heart. Continue in asking for whatever you need and rejoice in My provision. Forgiven sin is My great gift to humanity."

August 11

"And let the peace of God rule in your hearts, to the which you are called in one body; and be thankful." Colossians 3:15

"Not forsaking the assembling of ourselves together." Hebrews 10:25

Jesus said, "...freely you have received, freely give." Matthew 10:18

"Be careful for nothing; but in every thing by prayer and supplication with thanksgiving let your requests be made known unto God." Philippians 4:6

"Go. Be at peace. I am there with you like an overseeing parent. Gather with My people. Pour My love freely. Be a part of My living Body. Have no concern for tomorrow."

August 12

"...by love serve one another." Galatians 5:13

We are changed "from glory to glory, even as by the Spirit of the Lord." II Corinthians 3:18

"The effectual fervent prayer of a righteous man avails much." James 5:16

"...the Lord will hear when I call unto Him." Psalm 4:3

"My servants of love work with Me to right wrongs and change people for the better. This is genuine success. Be encouraged as I see and hear every prayer. Hope and trust."

August 13

Jesus said, "Inasmuch as you have done it unto one of the least of these My brethren, you have done it unto Me."
Matthew 25:40

Jesus said, "I am among you as He that serves." Luke 22:27

"You yourselves are taught of God to love one another." 1 Thessalonians 4:9

Jesus said, "These things have I spoken unto you, that My joy might remain in you, and that your joy might be full."
John 15:11

"Remember, when you serve the least, you serve Me. Carry on with joy in your inner life with Me as you perform the lowliest tasks for those in need. Thereby your joy is endlessly increased and warms the hearts of many. Encourage My best in others. I see and understand all."

August 14

"Grace be with you, and peace, from God our Father, and the Lord Jesus Christ." 1 Thessalonians 1:1

"Holy, holy, holy is the Lord of hosts: the whole earth is full of His glory." Isaiah 6:3

"My heart is fixed, O God, my heart is fixed: I will sing and give praise." Psalm 57:7

"To appoint unto them that mourn in Zion, to give them beauty for ashes, the oil of joy for mourning, the garment of praise for the spirit of heaviness; that they might be called trees of righteousness, the planting of the Lord, that He might be glorified." Isaiah 61: 3

"Go in grace amid the tumult of the world. All around is My glory, My creation. Recognize it and keep your heart stayed on Me. Thereby you will lift many a heavy, questioning heart."

August 15

Jesus said, "Again I say unto you, That if two of you shall agree on earth as touching anything that they shall ask, it shall be done for them of My Father which is in Heaven." Matthew 18:19

"Endeavoring to keep the unity of the Spirit in the bond of peace." Ephesians 4:3

"So shall My Word be that goes forth out of My mouth: it shall not return unto Me void, but it shall accomplish that which I please, and it shall prosper in the thing whereto I sent it." Isaiah 55:11

"Let this mind be in you, which was also in Christ Jesus." Philippians 2:5

"Agree with Me. Agree with My Word and My Spirit. The unity of hearts and minds avails much."

August 16

"From the end of the earth will I cry unto You, when my heart is overwhelmed: lead me to the rock that is higher than I." Psalm 61:2

"He heals the broken in heart, and binds up their wounds." Psalm 147:3

"And in the morning, rising up a great while before day, He went out, and departed into a solitary place, and there prayed." Mark 1:35

"And God shall wipe away all tears from their eyes; and there shall be no more death, neither sorrow, nor crying, neither shall there be any more pain: for the former things are passed away." Revelation 21:4

"Take My rest and peace in and around you. Withdraw with Me, away from the world's turmoil and demands. Be yourself, with nothing to prove and no role to uphold. Come close and allow Me to cover and heal all disappointments and distresses. Be assured, I will one day take away all tears and pain."

August 17

"Beloved, I wish above all things that you may prosper and be in health, even as your soul prospers." III John 2

"For I will restore health unto you, and I will heal you of your wounds, says the Lord." Jeremiah 30:17

"Blessed be the Lord, who daily loads us with benefits, even the God of our salvation." Psalm 68:19

"Bless the Lord, O my soul, and forget not all His benefits. Who forgives all your iniquities; who heals all your diseases." Psalm 103:2-3

"Freely receive of My health-giving wholeness in the sunshine, air, and natural surroundings. What I create is real and has ongoing benefits for you. Avoid the deceptive, manipulated amusements created by man."

August 18

"The Lord is neigh unto them that are of a broken heart; and saves such as be of a contrite spirit." Psalm 34:18

"My son, despise not the chastening of the Lord; neither be weary of His correction: for whom the Lord loves He corrects; even as a Father the son in whom He delights." Proverbs 3:11-12

"Behold, happy is the man whom God corrects: therefore despise not you the chastening of the Almighty." Job 5:17

Jesus said, "Likewise, I say unto you, there is joy in the presence of the angels of God over one sinner that repents." Luke 15:10

"Conviction of sin, of wrong thinking, is My love correcting what will only bring sorrow and loss to you. Receive My correction with thankfulness and repent at once."

August 19

"Wisdom is the principle thing; therefore get wisdom: and with all your getting get understanding." Proverbs 4:7

"Open You mine eyes, that I may behold wondrous things out of Your Law." Psalm 119:18

Jesus said, "But the hour comes, and now is, when the true worshippers shall worship the Father in spirit and in truth: for "...the Father seeks such to worship Him" John 4:23

"You shall love your neighbor as yourself." Mark 12:31

"Get wisdom. Out of all your experiences, get wisdom. I give revelations and answers to life in a way you can understand and act on, if needed. When your eyes are opened to My ways, your heart will worship Me in spirit and in truth, and your love for yourself and your neighbor will grow."

August 20

We, "being justified freely by His grace through the redemption that is in Christ Jesus." Romans 3:24

"For I will be merciful to their unrighteousness, and their sins and iniquities will I remember no more." Hebrews 8:12

Jesus said, "Verily I say unto you, Whosoever shall not receive the Kingdom of God as a little child shall in no wise enter therein." Luke 18:17

Jesus said, "I have glorified You on the earth: I have finished the work which You gave Me to do." John 17:4

"I am your total redemption for body, soul, and spirit. Everyday is a new beginning with Me. I don't remember your past sins, failures, and weaknesses. So, why should you trouble yourself about them or about those of others? Be as a little child who faces each day with wonder and interest. I am the guardian of your life, now and into eternity. My inheritance for you is joyful dependence on My finished work on the Cross."

August 21

"For you were sometimes darkness, but now are you light in the Lord: walk as children of light." Ephesians 5:8

"...let us lay aside every weight, and the sin which does so easily beset us, and let us run with patience the race that is set before us." Hebrews 12:1

Jesus said, "Hitherto have you asked nothing in My Name: ask, and you shall receive, that your joy may be full." John 16:24

"Every good and every perfect gift is from above, and comes down from the Father of lights, with whom is no variableness, neither shadow of turning." James 1:17

"Yes, child, keep your heart light as you walk the journey with Me. It does indeed give you a deep influence. Many will take note and wonder and ask how can this be? Let others see and hear that everything good they desire comes from Me."

August 22

"The Lord will be the hope of His people, and the strength of the children of Israel." Joel 3:16

"For I am the Lord, I change not." Malachi 3:6

"And you shall seek Me, and find Me, when you shall search for Me with all your heart." Jeremiah 29:13

"Till we all come in the unity of the faith, and of the knowledge of the Son of God, unto a perfect man, unto the measure of the stature of the fullness of Christ." Ephesians 4:13

"Place your hope in Me. You will not be disappointed. I do not waver or change. I can be known by those who seek Me with their whole heart. I bring stability and security to My children. I grow them up to follow Me."

August 23

"According to the eternal purpose which He purposed in Christ Jesus our Lord." Ephesians 3:11

"Therefore my beloved brethren, be you stedfast, unmoveable, always abounding in the work of the Lord, forasmuch as you know that your labor is not in vain in the Lord." 1 Corinthians 15:58

"And be not conformed to this world: but be you transformed by the renewing of your mind, that you may prove what is that good, and acceptable, and perfect will of God." Romans 12:2

"My people shall be satisfied with My goodness, says the Lord." Jeremiah 31:14

"Focus on My eternal purposes in your life and in the lives of others. Work with Me in the process of lifting and transforming lives for eternity. This is the labor I call you to, and this is where you will find deepest satisfaction and joy."

August 24

"But they that wait upon the Lord shall renew their strength; they shall mount up with wings as eagles; they shall run, and not be weary; and they shall walk, and not faint." Isaiah 40:31

"God is faithful, by whom you were called unto the fellowship of His Son Jesus Christ our Lord." 1 Corinthians 1:9

"They shall call on My Name, and I will hear them: I will say, It is My people: and they will say, The Lord is My God." Zechariah 13:9

"...our sufficiency is of God." II Corinthians 3:5

"Wait upon Me to renew your strength, to lift your burdens. I am with you in quiet companionship. I understand the trials of your patience and perseverance. My Spirit carries you through when you call upon Me. It is by My Spirit that you daily overcome all tests. Believe I am sufficient to every need."

August 25

"But I keep under my body, and bring it into subjection: lest that by any means, when I have preached to others, I myself should be a castaway." 1 Corinthians 9:27

"Order my steps in Your Word and let not any iniquity have dominion over me." Psalm 119:133

"...the simplicity that is in Christ." II Corinthians 11:3

Jesus said, "For whosoever shall do the will of God, the same is My brother, and My sister, and mother." Mark 3:35

"Yes, discipline your flesh and soul. Keep them under divine direction. Stay with My order, plan, and simplicity of life. Keep your will in line with Mine."

August 26

"Come you yourselves apart into a desert place, and rest awhile." Mark 6:31

"The Lord is my shepherd; I shall not want. He makes me to lie down in green pastures: He leads me beside the still waters." Psalm 23:1-2

Jesus said, "But rather seek you the Kingdom of God; and all these things shall be added unto you." Luke 12:31

"For the Kingdom of God is not meat and drink; but righteousness, and peace, and joy in the Holy Ghost." Romans 14:17

"Wait upon Me. Take time away from the pressure of doing to be with Me, quiet, resting, listening. I will restore your peace, your life energy, and your hope. It is My joy to do this. Those who live in My Kingdom have access to Me and all My goodness, caring for their needs."

August 27

"We should not trust in ourselves, but in God which raises the dead." II Corinthians 1:9

"I lead in the way of righteousness, in the midst of the paths of judgment." Proverbs 8:20

"For My thoughts are not your thoughts, neither are your ways My ways, says the Lord. For as the heavens are higher than the earth, so are My ways higher than your ways, and My thoughts than your thoughts." Isaiah 55:8-9

"Without counsel purposes are disappointed: but in the multitude of counsellors they are established." Proverbs 15:22

"Trust Me when you don't understand My leading. My thoughts, plans, and outcomes are past your understanding. Yield and be available and useable. Receive help and counsel from those going before you."

August 28

"And the servant of the Lord must not strive; but be gentle unto all men, apt to teach, patient." II Timothy 2:24

"Follow peace with all men, and holiness, without which no man shall see the Lord." Hebrews 12:14

God *"changes the times and the seasons."* Daniel 2:21

"For thus says the Lord God, the Holy One of Israel; in returning and rest shall you be saved; in quietness and in confidence shall be your strength." Isaiah 30:15

"Rest and peace are what I have for you. No pressure, no striving ambition. My goals are laid out by My timing. In this season of your life, quiet trust in Me accomplishes all that is needed."

August 29

"My sheep hear My voice, and I know them, and they follow Me." John 10:27

"Finally, brethren, whatsoever things are true, whatsoever things are honest, whatsoever things are just, whatsoever things are pure, whatsoever things are lovely, whatsoever things are of good report; if there be any virtue, and if there be any praise, think on these things." Philippians 4:8

"Submit yourselves therefore to God. Resist the devil, and he will flee from you." James 4:7

"The angel of the Lord encamps round about them that fear Him and delivers them." Psalm 34:7

"Hear Me speaking to you. Listen to My voice alone. I lead you only to what is true and good by My Spirit. Silence, rebuke, and flee from all other voices. It's My clarity and closeness that you will recognize, and My helping angels you will experience."

August 30

"For this cause I bow my knees unto the Father of our Lord Jesus Christ, of whom the whole family in Heaven and earth is named." Ephesians 3:14-15

God said of the Jewish nation Israel, "And I will make of you a great nation, and I will bless you, and make your name great; and you shall be a blessing: and I will bless them that bless you, and curse him that curses you: and in you shall all families of the earth be blessed." Genesis 12:2-3

"And he shall turn the heart of the fathers to the children, and the heart of the children to their fathers, lest I come and smite the earth with a curse." Malachi 4:6

"For you are all the children of God by faith in Christ Jesus." Galatians 3:26

"Family is My idea and My creation. I desire a family, and family is My way to show and teach who I am. Sorrowfully, many misunderstand, rebel, and reject their family and My family. My Spirit is at work to restore and draw My family together—those who in unity and agreement on earth recognize Me as their loving Father."

August 31

"Pray without ceasing. In everything give thanks: for this is the will of God in Christ Jesus concerning you."
II Thessalonians 5:17

Jesus said, "Whosoever will come after Me, let him deny himself, take up his cross and follow Me." Mark 8:34

"And it shall come to pass in the last days, says God, I will pour out My Spirit upon all flesh." Acts 2:17

*Jesus said, "Verily I say unto you, Whosoever shall not receive the Kingdom of God as a little child,
he shall not enter therein."* Mark 10:15

"Yes, constancy in communion with Me, and denying yourself, enable My Spirit to pour through you abundant goodness in many forms. You will be intent on Me, and My intentions will be realized without your concern or even knowledge. This is childlike living in My grace."

September

September 1

"But we have the mind of Christ." 1 Corinthians 2:16

"The lines are fallen unto me in pleasant places; yes, I have a goodly heritage." Psalm 16:6

"For the earth is the Lord's, and the fullness thereof." 1 Corinthians 10:26

"O the depth of the riches both of the wisdom and knowledge of God! how unsearchable are His judgments, and His ways past finding out! Romans 11:33

"Survey your surroundings with My mind, the mind of Christ. Have I not placed you in a pleasant place? What you see flourishing in abundant provision and care is of My glory. I hold the earth in My hands; I order it's turning. My love for you is past your comprehending."

September 2

"If God be for us, who can be against us?" Romans 8:31

Jesus said, "Because straight is the gate, and narrow is the way, which leads unto life, and few there be that find it."
Matthew 7:14

"But let all those that put their trust in You rejoice: let them ever shout for joy, because You defend them."
Psalm 5:11

"For we know Him that has said, Vengeance belongs to Me, I will recompense, says the Lord." Hebrews 10:30

"Have no fear for what man can do or say against you. Keep pressing on My narrow path that leads to life. I am your defender, your vindicator."

September 3

"I am the Lord that heals you." Exodus 15:26

"And I will restore to you the years that the locust has eaten." Joel 2:25

"Many are the afflictions of the righteous: but the Lord delivers him out of them all." Psalm 34:19

Jesus said, "In the world you shall have tribulation: but be of good cheer; I have overcome the world." John 16:33

"Know I am with you to heal and restore. There is much that could afflict you in the world, but I overcome in you all that seeks to harm you."

September 4

"…he went on his way rejoicing." Acts 8:39

Jesus said, "Rejoice, because your names are written in Heaven." Luke 10:20

Jesus said, "Take heed that you be not deceived." Luke 21:8

"Be you also patient; establish your hearts: for the coming of the Lord draws nigh." James 5:8

"Yes, go your way rejoicing. Your name is written in My book. I see, I understand the price you pay to follow Me; and know it is the only investment you need to make. Many are investing and trusting in deception. Have no fear or worry. I am coming for My own."

September 5

Jesus said, "But I say unto you which hear, Love your enemies, do good to them which hate you." Luke 6:27

Jesus said, "Give and it shall be given unto you; good measure, pressed down, and shaken together, and running over, shall men give into your bosom. For with the same measure that you give out it shall be measured to you again." Luke 6:38

"He that spared not His own Son, but delivered Him up for us all, how shall He not with Him also freely give us all things." Romans 8:32

"If any man thirst, let him come unto Me and drink. He that believes on Me, as the Scripture has said, out of his belly shall flow rivers of Living Water." John 7:37-38

"Yes, My life is in giving. I fill your heart more deeply and abundantly as you pour out My love in many ways. Look not for return and give without expectation or control. Freely give as it has been freely and abundantly given to you."

September 6

"And, lo, the angel of the Lord came upon them, and the glory of the Lord shown round about them." Luke 2:9

"The heart of him that has understanding seeks knowledge." Proverbs 15:14

Jesus said, "Howbeit when He, the Spirit of truth, is come, He will guide you into all truth." John 16:13

Jesus said, "Whosoever comes to Me, and hears My sayings, and does them, I will show you to whom he is like: he is like a man which builds a house, and digs deep, and laid the foundation on a rock: and when the flood arose, the stream beat vehemently upon that house, and could not shake it, for it was founded upon a rock." Luke 6:47-48

"There is much of My ways you cannot comprehend on your side of Heaven. I work, My angels work, and to a smaller extent, My children work. All together, it is an intricate inter-relatedness, unfathomable to you. You must trust Me as a loving, all knowing Father. I gave My Spirit as your Guide and He reveals and leads in all that is necessary for you to know and do. Hear, obey, and trust My Holy, Perfect Spirit."

September 7

"I will say of the Lord, He is my refuge and my fortress: My God; in Him will I trust." Psalm 91:2

"You are my hiding place; You shall preserve me from trouble." Psalm 32:7

"This know also, that in the last days perilous times shall come." II Timothy 3:1

"Fear not, nor be dismayed, be strong and of good courage." Joshua 10:25

"Yes, I am your safe hiding place, sure and ever with you. Make Me known to all around you, for times of great trouble will sweep the earth. Many will fall for lack of My safe hiding place. It's a time to draw your courage and protection from Me and be prepared."

September 8

"...the joy of the Lord is your strength." Nehemiah 8:10

"I will greatly rejoice in the Lord, my soul shall be joyful in my God; for He has clothed me with the garments of salvation, He has covered me with the robe of righteousness." Isaiah 61:10

"...he that is of a merry heart has a continual feast." Proverbs 15:15

"For by grace are you saved through faith; and that not of yourselves: it is the gift of God." Ephesians 2:8

"My joy in you is real and strengthening and noticed, especially, by those who do not know Me and trust Me. It puts the bounce in your step, the openness to fun and spontaneity. It motivates you to generosity. It silently advertises Me and My gifts."

September 9

"Your faithfulness is unto all generations: You have established the earth, and it abides." Psalm 119: 90

"...their soul shall be as a watered garden." Jeremiah 31:12

Jesus said, "Go you therefore, and teach all nations, baptizing them in the Name of the Father, and of the Son, and of the Holy Ghost: Teaching them to observe all things whatsoever I have commanded you: and, lo, I am with you always, even unto the end of the world." Matthew 28:19-20

"For the vineyard of the Lord of hosts is the house of Israel, and the men of Judah his pleasant plant." Isaiah 5:7

"Faithful, faithful, faithful. I am faithful. No matter the circumstances about you, remain faithful to Me, to those around you and to what I have called you to. Continue to nurture and disciple the older relationships. My healing requires time and oversight as a gardener over his garden. Be faithful to the work I've called you to and cast all other cares on Me. I am the Master Gardener."

September 10

"Now the God of hope fill you with all joy and peace in believing, that you may abound in hope, through the power of the Holy Ghost." Romans 15:13

Jesus said, "Behold, I stand at the door, and knock: if any man hear My voice, and open the door, I will come in to him, and will sup with him, and he with Me." Revelation 3:20

"I set my face like a flint, and I know that I shall not be ashamed." Isaiah 50:7

"And they remembered that God was their rock, and the high God their redeemer." Psalm 78:35

"I want to be and need to be the influencer in your life. Keep your inner life with Me flourishing, hear My voice, consider My Words. Remain steady in this when other influences, voices, and pressures come from the outer world. Remember, your house is established on Me, the unchanging rock."

September 11

"But we all, with open faces beholding as in a glass the glory of the Lord, are changed into the same image from glory to glory, even as by the Spirit of the Lord." II Corinthians 3:18

"…to be conformed to the image of His son." Romans 8:29

"Those things which you have both learned and received, and heard, and seen in me, do: and the God of peace shall be with you." Philippians 4:9

"I press toward the mark for the prize of the high calling of God in Christ Jesus." Philippians 3:14

"You cannot change yourself. By sharing in My life and in the lives of those who know My character, are you changed to My character. The world is a place of learning for your transformation back to Me. This is My loving purpose and your goal."

September 12

Jesus said, "But rather seek you the Kingdom of God; and all these things shall be added unto you." Luke 12:31

"For we dare not make ourselves of the number, or compare ourselves with some that commend themselves."
II Corinthians 10:12

Jesus said, "These things have I spoken unto you, that My joy might remain in you, and that your joy might be full."
John 15:11

Jesus said, "But even the very hairs of your head are all numbered. Fear not therefore:
you are of more value than many sparrows." Luke 12:7

"Set your heart upon My Kingdom purposes. Use the gifts I've given you without comparison with others. I offer you individually prepared fulfillment and joy in this. No one else can take or give you this. Only I know the full value and outcome of each life. Observe, enjoy, and obey Me."

September 13

"Neither is there salvation in any other: for there is none other Name under heaven given among men, whereby we must be saved." Acts 4:12

"...but you are washed, but you are sanctified, but you are justified in the Name of the Lord Jesus, and by the Spirit of our God." II Corinthians 6:11

"Pray one for another, that you may be healed." James 5:16

"Let all those that seek You rejoice and be glad in You: let such as love Your salvation say continually, The Lord be magnified." Psalm 40:16

"There is no other Name under Heaven whereby you can be saved. It's My joy to save, to rescue, to restore. Invite Me into the lives of others by prayer. Look, and find Me everywhere."

September 14

"The righteous shall flourish like the palm tree: he shall grow like a cedar in Lebanon. Those that be planted in the house of the Lord shall flourish in the courts of our God. They shall bring forth fruit in old age; they shall be fat and flourishing." Psalm 92:12-14

"Though our outward man perish, yet the inward man is renewed day by day." II Corinthians 4:16

"He that watereth shall be watered also himself." Proverbs 11:25

The Godly "shall be like a tree planted by the rivers of water, that brings forth his fruit in his season; his leaf also shall not wither; and whatsoever he does shall prosper." Psalm 1:3

"Old age is a gift, enabling you to experience more, learn more, and do more for Me. Even without much outer activity, much can be accomplished in the unseen spiritual realm. Do not be discouraged looking at your outer person. Relish the building up and giving out of greater living waters from within. These can be the richest, most productive years—truly golden years."

September 15

"He is the living God, and steadfast forever, and His Kingdom that which shall not be destroyed, and His dominion shall be even unto the end." Daniel 6:26

"And they rejected His statutes, and His covenant that He made with their fathers, and His testimonies which He testified against them; and they followed vanity, and became vain, and went after the heathen that were round about them, concerning whom the Lord had charged them, that they should not do like them." II Kings 17:15

"His head and His hairs were white like wool, as white as snow; and His eyes were as a flame of fire." Revelation 1:14

"Bless the Lord, O my soul: and all that is within me, bless His holy Name. Bless the Lord, O my soul, and forget not all His benefits: who forgives all your iniquities; who heals all your diseases; who redeems your life from destruction; who crowns you with loving kindness and tender mercies; who satisfies your mouth with good things; so that your youth is renewed like the eagle's." Psalm 103:1-5

"I am with you, unchanging, in every season of your life. Be not troubled by the vanities of this present age. Your white hairs speak of length of days and experience, as well as service to Me and others. Let your youthful spirit spring forth to lift others. There is timeless beauty and grace in My holiness."

September 16

Jesus said, "In My Father's house are many mansions: if it were not so, I would have told you. I go to prepare a place for you." John 14:2

"My son, forget not My law; but let your heart keep My commandments: For length of days, and long life, and peace, shall they add to you." Proverbs 3:1-2

"And we know that all things work together for good to them that love God, to them who are the called according to His purpose." Romans 8:28

"And the work of righteousness shall be peace; and the effect of righteousness quietness and assurance forever." Isaiah 32:17

"I plan your life and your seasons. Have My peace concerning your effectiveness and length of days. I hear your prayers and your concerns for the future. Trust that much is working in the unseen world as I bring all interweavings of life together. Rest in hope of Me and My overseeing wisdom."

September 17

"Heal me, O Lord, and I shall be healed; save me, and I shall be saved: for you are my praise." Jeremiah 17:14

"Restore unto me the joy of Your salvation; and uphold me with Your free Spirit." Psalm 51:12

"For the Lord gives wisdom: out of His mouth comes knowledge and understanding." Proverbs 2:6

"You will guide me with your counsel, and afterward receive me to glory." Psalm 73:24

"Healing and restoration are My outpouring love to My children. They hear My voice of wisdom answering their cries. Rest and quiet are needed to hear My guiding Words. I only say what will bring life."

September 18

"Whosoever shall receive one of such children in My Name, receives Me: and whosoever shall receive Me, receives not Me, but Him that sent Me." Mark 9:37

"Blessed are the poor in spirit: for theirs is the Kingdom of Heaven." Matthew 5:3

Jesus said, "You say that I am a king. To this end was I born, and for this cause came I into the world, that I should bear witness unto the truth. Everyone that is of the truth hears My voice." John 18:37

Jesus said, "For God so loved the world, that He gave His only begotten Son, that whosoever believes in Him should not perish, but have everlasting life." John 3:16

"Remember the little ones, the overlooked, rejected, and poor in spirit ones. I came for these and I send you to these ones. Make it known that I and My rich, true Kingdom are available to all who seek Me faithfully. I want none to perish."

September 19

But you shall receive power after that the Holy Ghost has come upon you." Acts 1:8

"Now we have received not the spirit of the world, but the Spirit which is of God; that we might know the things which are freely given to us of God." 1 Corinthians 2:12

"Let us come before His presence with thanksgiving, and make a joyful noise unto Him with psalms." Psalm 95:2

"But he that received seed unto the good ground is he that hears the Word, and understands it; which also bears fruit, and brings forth, some an hundred fold, some sixty, some thirty." Matthew 13:23

"Receive, receive, receive with joy and thanksgiving every moment of life's experiences. Find Me and My handiwork in all situations and people. Therein lies a rich and meaningful life bearing continuous fruit."

September 20

"…your sons and your daughters shall prophesy, your old men shall dream dreams, your young men shall see visions." Joel 2:28

Jesus said, "I am Alpha and Omega, the beginning and the end, the first and last." Revelation 22:13

"A prudent man foresees the evil, and hides himself." Proverbs 22:3

"The Name of the Lord is a strong tower: the righteous runs in to it, and is safe." Proverbs 18:10

"Yes, I speak to My children in dreams, and visions. I arrest their attention in this way so they do not doubt Me. I know the past, present, and future and desire to reveal My will clearly. In this way, much trouble is averted and My protection is sure."

September 21

"In the beginning God created the heaven and the earth." Genesis 1:1

"My soul follows hard after You: Your right hand upholds me." Psalm 63:8

"For we know in part, and we prophesy in part." 1 Corinthians 13:9

"You open Your hand, and satisfy the desire of every living thing." Psalm 145:16

"Yes, I am the Creator and sustainer of the universe, and as you know Me, as limited as it is in your human condition, other desires lose their attraction and power. I alone truly satisfy."

September 22

"I will sing unto the Lord, because He has dealt bountifully with me." Psalm 13:6

"But the very hairs of your head are all numbered." Matthew 10:30

"…choose you this day whom you will serve…but as for me and my house, we will serve the Lord" Joshua 24:15

"No servant can serve two masters: for either he will hate the one, and love the other; or else he will hold to the one, and despise the other. You cannot serve God and mammon." Luke 16:13

"Look around you; am I not bountiful in all I do and create? Who will count the leaves or the hairs of your head? Choose My life of righteousness, peace, and joy in My Spirit's leading. Leave the money god to the sad, lonely ones who refuse Me."

September 23

Jesus said, "For whosoever exalts himself shall be abased; and he that humbles himself shall be exalted." Luke 14:11

"The fear of the Lord is the beginning of wisdom: and the knowledge of the holy is understanding." Proverbs 9:10

Jesus said, "Peace I leave with you, My peace I give unto you: not as the world gives, give I unto you. Let not your heart be troubled, neither let it be afraid." John 14:27

"And God is able to make all grace abound toward you; that you, always having all sufficiency in all things, may abound to every good work." II Corinthians 9:8

"There's a beauty that only comes from humble holiness. Wanting what I want calms the troubled, searching heart. In exchange for all of you, I give everything of Me."

September 24

"Praise Him for His mighty acts: praise Him according to His excellent greatness." Psalm 150:2

"For I reckon that the sufferings of this present time are not worthy to be compared with the glory which shall be revealed in us." Romans 8:18

"...we must through much tribulation enter into the Kingdom of God." Acts 14:22

"Though He were a Son, yet learned He obedience by the things which He suffered." Hebrews 5:8

"Gratitude, thankful praise, and sincere understanding that sees Me in everything, this is the attitude of My children. This includes suffering needed to learn obedience. O, that I had more prophetic ones who understand the nature of suffering, My nature as a wise Father."

September 25

"How much more shall your Heavenly Father give the Holy Spirit to them that ask Him?" Luke 11:13

"If we live in the Spirit, let us also walk in the Spirit." Galatians 5:25

"But God has revealed them unto us by His Spirit: for the Spirit searches all things, yes, the deep things of God." 1 Corinthians 2:10

"Know you not that your body is the temple of the Holy Ghost which is in you, which you have of God, and you are not your own?" 1 Corinthians 6:19

"I am the perfect Holy Spirit. I desire to abide with you as your closest companion. I want you to experience your life in continuous, practical communion with Me. I know everything. When you speak with Me and act with Me, you know, experience, and follow My flow of true living, the joy of living."

172

September 26

"Jesus laid aside His garments; and took a towel, and girded Himself. After that He poured water into a basin, and began to wash the disciple's feet, and to wipe them with the towel." John 13:4-5

"And as you would that men should do to you, do you also to them likewise." Luke 6:31

"And whatsoever you do in word or deed, do all in the Name of the Lord Jesus, giving thanks to God and the Father by Him." Colossians 3:17

Jesus said, "I say unto you, inasmuch as you have done it unto one of the least of these My brothers, you have done it unto Me." Matthew 25:40

"Yes, take up the towel of service, as I did. Be as I am to others. Anticipate needs to fill and joy to bring. Participate with Me in bringing genuine care to others. Any work of goodness is worthwhile. Be free of all pride and selfishness to bless others in My Name and Spirit."

September 27

Lead me in Your truth, and teach me: for You are the God of my salvation; on You do I wait all the day." Psalm 25:5

"Study to show yourself approved unto God, a workman that needs not to be ashamed, rightly dividing the Word of truth." II Timothy 2:15

Jesus said, "Take My yoke upon you, and learn of Me; for I am meek and lowly in heart: and you shall find rest unto your souls." Matthew 11:29

"Examine yourselves, whether you be in the faith; prove your own selves." II Corinthians 13:5

"Learning, ever learning is the condition of My children. Some lessons must be repeated to eliminate pride, arrogance, and self-sufficiency. My patience is limitless, but My desire to save is also endless. Be quick to examine yourself for the needed transformation I am calling for. Be good students."

September 28

"That you be not soon shaken in mind, or be troubled, neither by spirit, nor by word, nor by letter as from us, as that the day of Christ is at hand." II Thessalonians 2:2

Jesus said, "Peace I leave with you, my peace I give unto you: not as the world giveth, give I unto you. Let not your heart be troubled, neither let it be afraid." John 14:27

"That the God of our Lord Jesus Christ, the Father of glory, may give unto you the spirit of wisdom and revelation in the knowledge of Him." Ephesians 1:17

Jesus said, "Let not your heart be troubled: you believe in God, believe also in Me." John 14:1

"Don't be troubled by small disappointments and evil tidings. I create an oasis of peace where My thoughts and revelations hold fast. I show you how to respond in ways that bring My protection and My peace. Let not your heart be troubled."

September 29

"And the Lord shall guide you continually, and satisfy your soul in drought, and make fat your bones: and you shall be like a watered garden, and like a spring of water, whose waters fail not. And they that shall be of thee shall build the old waste places: you shall raise up the foundations of many generations; and you shall be called, The repairer of the breach, The restorer of paths to dwell in." Isaiah 58:11-12

"Trust in the Lord with all your heart; and lean not unto your own understanding. In all your ways acknowledge Him, and He shall direct your paths." Proverbs 3:5-6

"I am God and there is none like Me, declaring the end from the beginning, and from ancient times the things that are not yet done, saying, My counsel shall stand, and I will do all My pleasure." Isaiah 46:9-10

Jesus said, "If you then, being evil, know how to give good gifts unto your children: how much more shall your Heavenly Father give the Holy Spirit to them that ask Him?" Luke 11:13

"I desire the transformation of My people more than you do. Be comforted that I wait and do not give up hope for each one. As always, do not lean to your understanding, but trust I know best. I see the end and I know what each one needs. I am a nurturing Father."

September 30

"But know that the Lord has set apart him that is Godly for Himself: the Lord will hear when I call unto Him."
Psalm 4:3

"For He knows our frame; He remembers that we are dust." Psalm 103:14

"...our fellowship is with the Father, and with His Son Jesus Christ." 1 John 1:3

"In the day when I cried You answered me, and strengthened me with strength in my soul." Psalm 138:3

"Yes, trust Me to hear and answer your cries and requests. Your part is to hear and see My response, and to do your part to receive the best outcome. I understand your human weaknesses and dilemmas. Choose My way diligently in quiet fellowship with Me. I always give answers to My children who wait in trust."

October

October 1

"Blessed be God, even the Father of our Lord Jesus Christ, the Father of mercies, and the God of all comfort." II Corinthians 1:3

"For do I now persuade men, or God? or do I seek to please men? For if I yet pleased men, I should not be the servant of Christ. Galatians 1:10

Wisdom "is more precious than rubies: and all the things you can desire are not to be compared unto her." Proverbs 3:15

"But covet earnestly the best gifts: and yet shew I unto you a more excellent way." 1 Corinthians 12:31

"I give you the inner comfort in times of outer pressure. I use you to touch and reach others in ways you cannot fully understand. Cease to evaluate yourself and compare yourself with others. My call, My work through you is unique. Take my comfort and rejoice that I use your unique gifts for My good pleasure and outcomes."

October 2

Jesus said, "…whosoever will be great among you, let him be your minister." Matthew 20:26 (NASB)

Jesus said, "Blessed are the meek: for they shall inherit the earth." Matthew 5:5

"That you may with one mind and one mouth glorify God, even the Father of our Lord Jesus Christ." Romans 15:6

"Great peace have they which love Your Law: and nothing shall offend them." Psalm 119:165

"True leaders are the meek. Those who yield to My gentle, strong voice and hand. Those who make My thoughts their thoughts. Those who love My Law have no need to be offended."

October 3

The Lord shall reign forever, even your God, O Zion, unto all generations. Praise the Lord." Psalm 146:10

"And that you study to be quiet, and to do your own business, and to work with your own hands, as we commanded you." 1 Thessalonians 4:11

"Be you therefore followers of God, as dear children." Ephesians 5:1

"we trust in the living God, who is the Saviour of all men." 1 Timothy 4:10

"Let My spirit reign. Let Me lead. Quietness and calmness are My way. You are My child and My child must trust My greatness."

October 4

"So we fasted and besought our God for this: and He was intreated of us." Ezra 8:23

"Incline your ear, O Lord, and hear; open your eyes, O Lord and see." Isaiah 37:17

"Surely the Lord God will do nothing, but He reveals His secret unto His servants the prophets." Amos 3:7

Jesus said, "You should love your neighbor as yourself." Matthew 19:19

"Fast and pray. Concentrate all your energies on hearing from Me. Know that I see all that concerns you of the happenings in your world. I show My prophetic people what must inevitably happen in the days ahead. Be one who agrees with My good will and care for My people."

October 5

"He shall call upon Me, and I will answer him: I will be with him in trouble; I will deliver him, and honour him. With long life will I satisfy him, and show him My salvation." Psalm 91:15-16

"Now no chastening for the present seems to be joyous, but grievous: nevertheless afterward it yields the peaceable fruit of righteousness unto them which are exercised thereby." Hebrews 12:11

"I have set before you life and death, blessing and cursing: therefore choose life, that both you and your seed may live." Deuteronomy 30:19

Jesus said, "It is written in the prophets, And they shall be all taught of God. Every man therefore that has heard, and has learned of the Father, comes unto Me." John 6:45

"All the events of your life have meaning and purpose. All are not pleasant. No chastening is joyous for the moment, but afterwards yields the peaceable fruit of righteousness. I allow you to choose life or death. Learn of Me, for this is My desire for you in your life's journey."

October 6

"My Beloved spoke, and said unto me, Rise up, My love, My fair one, and come away." Song Of Solomon 2:10

"Rest in the Lord, and wait patiently for Him." Psalm 37:7

"Six days shall work be done, but on the seventh day there shall be to you an holy day,
a sabbath of rest to the Lord." Exodus 35:2

Jesus said, "I and My Father are one." John 10:30

"Rest. Come away with Me to a quiet place and rest in Me. Even six days should you work, and then take a day of rest. I and My Son are one and I want you to experience the complete peace of oneness with Me."

October 7

"...and the peace of God, which passes all understanding, shall keep your hearts and minds through Christ Jesus." Philippians 4:7

"The thoughts of the diligent tend only to plenteousness." Proverbs 21:5

"For the Word of God is quick, and powerful, and sharper than any twoedged sword, piercing even to the dividing asunder of soul and spirit, and of the joints and marrow, and is a discerner of the thoughts and intents of the heart." Hebrews 4:12

"My sheep hear My voice, and I know them, and they follow Me." John 10:27

"Rest, My rest means more than inactivity. It means release of your thoughts to make a clear room for Mine. I am ever at work to change you by making My thoughts real to you. Know My quiet voice and commune with Me in deep rest. I too enjoy this.

October 8

"But now they desire a better country, that is, an Heavenly: wherefore God is not ashamed to be called their God: for He has prepared for them a city." Hebrews 11:16

"One thing have I desired of the Lord, that will I seek after; that I may dwell in the house of the Lord all the days of my life, to behold the beauty of the Lord, and to enquire in His temple." Psalm 27:4

Jesus said, "I am not sent but unto the lost sheep of the house of Israel." Matthew 15:24

"God is our refuge and strength, a very present help in trouble." Psalm 46:1

"Your true home is with Me. You have longed for, searched for, and found Me, your Saviour, your true home. Now, you are able to bring others to Me, to find they have a secure home, a refuge of acceptance, and a good Father."

October 9

"I am the vine, you are the branches. He that abides in Me, and I in him, the same brings forth much fruit: for without Me you can do nothing." John 15:5

"For we know in part, and we prophesy in part." 1 Corinthians 13:9

"God that made the world and all things therein, seeing that He is Lord of Heaven and earth, dwells not in temples made with hands." Acts 17:24

"And we have seen and do testify that the Father sent the Son to be the Saviour of the world." 1 John 4:14

"I am your source. I hold up the world in My hand. I am the energy that is required for all life. I am present everywhere. When you search to understand, you know only a small part of Me, but it is enough to show your place in the great universe. In humility and obedient listening, your spirit finds I am real."

October 10

"The Lord is righteous in all His ways, and holy in all His works." Psalm 145:17

"Your Word is a lamp unto my feet, and a light unto my path." Psalm 119:105

"We also joy in God through our Lord Jesus Christ, by whom we have now received the atonement." Romans 5:11

"Looking unto Jesus the author and finisher of our faith; who for the joy that was set before Him endured the Cross, despising the shame, and is set down at the right hand of the throne of God." Hebrews 12:2

"Attain fresh experience and knowledge of Me and My ways. Be ever attuned to My Word and My voice. Every problem on earth, every need is covered in My atoning work. The Cross is the center of every solution you need."

October 11

"But there is a God in Heaven that reveals secrets." Daniel 2:28

Jesus said, *"As long as I am in the world, I am the light of the world."* John 9:5

"Comfort you, comfort you My people, says your God." Isaiah 40:1

Jesus said, *"Take therefore no thought for the morrow: for the morrow shall take thought for the things of itself. Sufficient unto the day is the evil thereof."* Matthew 6:34

"Do not seek to interpret all the secrets of My prophets and My timing for these final days which trouble many. Better to bring My light and comfort to your present sphere of influence. I am seeking My people to be the generosity that pours from a deep, quiet trust in Me. This is sufficient for today."

October 12

"Let your moderation be known unto all men." Philippians 4:5

"But be you doers of the word, and not hearers only, deceiving your own selves." James 1:22

"The wicked flee when no man pursues: but the righteous are bold as a lion." Proverbs 28:1

"Confess your faults one to another, and pray one for another, that you may be healed." James 5:16

"Find a balance between introspection and action. Searching your heart for deep cleansing and repentance is good, but it must be in balance. Hear from Me, then boldly go forth into the fray. Center your life on Me and My truth, rather than excessive self-examination and emphasis on your faults."

October 13

"Moreover it is required in stewards, that a man be found faithful." 1 Corinthians 4:2

"For since the beginning of the world men have not heard, nor perceived by the ear, neither has the eye seen, O God, beside you, what He has prepared for him that waits for Him." Isaiah 64:4

"Therefore thus says the Lord God, Behold, I lay in Zion for a foundation a stone, a tried stone, a precious corner stone, a sure foundation: he that believes shall not make haste." Isaiah 28:16

"For God is not the author of confusion, but of peace, as in all churches of the saints." 1 Corinthians 14:33

"Steward My abundance. There will be time for all that I ask of you. Haste and confusion are not My usual means to lead to better things."

October 14

"Glory and honor are in His presence; strength and gladness are in His place." I Chronicles 16:27

"Cast your burden upon the Lord, and He shall sustain you: He shall never suffer the righteous to be moved." Psalm 55:22

"The Lord will give strength unto His people; The Lord will bless His people with peace." Psalm 29:11

"Delight yourself also in the Lord; and He shall give you the desires of your heart." Psalm 37:4

"Be comforted in My presence today. Release all the past concerns, and look to Me for peace today. In Heaven we just are. Time does not exist. Aim for a childlike delight in today's wonders, joys, and life."

October 15

"You will show me the path of life: in Your presence is fullness of joy; at Your right hand there are pleasures for evermore." Psalm 16:11

"You shall hide them in the secret of Your presence from the pride of man: You shall keep them secretly in a pavilion from the strife of tongues." Psalm 31:20

Jesus said, "Whosoever therefore shall humble himself as this little child, the same is greatest in the Kingdom of Heaven." Matthew 18:4

"You prepare a table before me in the presence of my enemies: You anoint my head with oil, my cup runs over." Psalm 23:5

"Fullness of joy. This is My desire for My sons and My daughters. It's available beyond your understanding. Come as a yielded, trusting child into the secret Spirit place with Me, your Heavenly Father. Know My accepting, transforming love, with a mindset of abundant fullness, overflowing."

October 16

Jesus said, "Judge not, that you be not judged. For with what judgment you judge, you shall be judged: and with what measure you mete, it shall be measured to you again." Matthew 7:1-2

Jesus said, "And why behold you the mote that is in your brother's eye, but consider not the beam that is in your own eye?" Matthew 7:3

Jesus said, "For the Son of man is come to save that which was lost." Matthew 18:11

"When I cry unto you, then shall my enemies turn back: this I know; for God is for me." Psalm 56:9

"Be aware of the beam in your own eye as you evaluate others. My value and love are upon all. Look to examine your own heart and motives and sin. Thereby you often do the greatest service to others. My love desires that not one would be lost. Remember, every journey to salvation is a unique story. Help and bless where I lead."

October 17

Jesus said, "I am the vine, you are the branches: He that abides in Me, and I in him, the same brings forth much fruit: for without Me you can do nothing." John 15:5

"For He satisfies the longing soul, and fills the hungry soul with goodness." Psalm 107:9

Jesus said, "He that finds his life shall lose it: and he that loses his life for My sake shall find it." Matthew 10:39

"Let your conversation be without covetousness; and be content with such things as you have: for He has said, I will never leave you, nor forsake you." Hebrews 13:5

"Abiding means you've settled the matter of holding to Me in all circumstances. I've become your place of peace and satisfaction. You look upon life from My vantage point and are content and not deceived. Godliness with contentment are truly great gain and sufficient success."

October 18

"Keep your heart with all diligence; for out of it are the issues of life." Proverbs 4:23

Jesus said, "If a man love Me, he will keep My Words: and My Father will love him, and We will come unto him, and make our abode with him." John 14:23

Jesus said, "For the bread of God is He which comes down from Heaven, and gives life unto the world." John 6:33

"Thus says God the Lord, He that created the heavens, and stretched them out; He that spread forth the earth, and that which comes out of it; He that gives breath unto the people upon it, and spirit to them that walk therein." Isaiah 42:5

"I say, do not judge because you cannot know another's heart as I do. Each has a complexity of joy and pain only I fully understand. When My outpouring love touches a heart, I am glad, hoping to know its return to Me. The universe operates on love given and received. To be a good receiver and giver is a great achievement; like breathing in and breathing out, it fosters life through the body, My Body."

October 19

"Now you are the Body of Christ, and members in particular." I Corinthians 12:27

God spoke, "That in blessing I will bless you, and in multiplying I will multiply your seed as the stars of the heaven, and as the sand which is upon the sea shore; and your seed shall possess the gate of his enemies." Genesis 22:17

"But the Word of God grew and multiplied." Acts 12:24

The Lord Jesus said, "I will never leave you nor forsake you." Hebrews 13:5

I build My community, My Body, My Kingdom, always growing, multiplying, extending over all the earth. None of man's foolishness, sin, and blindness hinders My creating and working. When you call and seek Me, I hear and reply. I am the ever present Father watching over My creation."

October 20

"A wise man will hear, and will increase learning; and a man of understanding shall attain unto wise counsels." Proverbs 1:5

"For You are my rock and my fortress; therefore for your Name's sake, lead me, and guide me." Psalm 31:3

Jesus said, "But the Comforter, which is the Holy Ghost, whom the Father will send in My Name, He shall teach you all things, and bring all things to your remembrance, whatsoever I have said unto you." John 14:26

Jesus said, "Truly, truly, I say unto you, Except a corn of wheat fall into the ground and die, it abides alone: but if it die, it brings forth much fruit." John 12:24

"There is always much to be learned as you follow the leading of My Spirit. Your life becomes an extraordinary adventure when your attitude is one of teachableness. Continue to die to your own opinions, prejudices and understandings. Become as a child, always imitating the Father."

October 21

"To the praise of the glory of His grace, wherein He has made us accepted in the beloved." Ephesians 1:6

"So God created man in His own image, in the image of God created He him; male and female created He them." Genesis 1:27

Jesus said, "Go you into all the world, and preach the Gospel to every creature." Mark 16:15

"Who is he that overcomes the world, but he that believes that Jesus is the Son of God?" 1 John 5:5

"I open My arms to the least of you. All are created by My love, even when hindered by sin and ignorance. Go as I have commanded. Go to those who are seeking, lost, and in need. Preach My Gospel. Lift and save the fallen ones. My truth prevails at the end of man's ideas and perversions. This is My overcoming love to all mankind. I don't pass any by."

October 22

"As every man has received the gift, even so minister the same one to another, as good stewards of the manifold grace of God." 1 Peter 4:10

"But you, beloved, building up yourselves on your most holy faith, praying in the Holy Ghost." Jude 20

"For as the body without the spirit is dead, so faith without works is dead also." James 2:26

"Be of good courage, and He shall strengthen your heart, all you that hope in the Lord." Psalm 31:24

"Faith, even My faith is a gift. Receive it with joyful thanks. Use it and pass it on. Sow it into others, especially the young, and tell them of My faithfulness. Make your faith real by what you show and say in the everyday, small events. With increasing faith, comes hope and My increasing love and courage. I am the God of limitless increase. Enjoy being part of it."

October 23

"For we walk by faith, not by sight." II Corinthians 5:7

"For by Him were all things created, that are in heaven, and that are in earth, visible and invisible, whether they be thrones, or dominions, or principalities, or powers: all things were created by Him, and for Him." Colossians 1:16

"Meditate upon these things; give yourself wholly to them; that your profiting may appear to all." 1 Timothy 4:15

"A faithful man shall abound with blessings: but he that makes haste to be rich shall not be innocent." Proverbs 28:20

"Gently walk with Me through each day's challenges and needs. Experience wonder and appreciation of all I have created and am continually doing. Receive My thoughts, taking time to meditate on My Words. Those who push and pull in haste through their life will miss My riches."

October 24

"Now the Spirit speaks expressly, that in the latter times some shall depart from the faith, giving heed to seducing spirits, and doctrines of devils." 1 Timothy 4:1

"The steps of a good man are ordered by the Lord: and he delights in His way." Psalm 37:23

"Keep me as the apple of the eye, hide me under the shadow of your wings." Psalm 17:8

"Rejoice in the Lord always: and again I say Rejoice." Philippians 4:4

"Yes, the times are evil with much corruption and confusion. But, My people and My plan continue to proceed under My hand and ordered time. Fear not. Look to your shelter under My wing. Rejoice and bring My power to bear where you are. I am still your refuge."

October 25

"O Lord, correct me, but with judgment; not in your anger, lest You bring me to nothing." Jeremiah 10:24

"Submitting yourselves one to another in the fear of God." Ephesians 5:21

"But the fruit of the Spirit is love, joy, peace, longsuffering, gentleness, goodness, faith, meekness, temperance: against such there is no law." Galatians 5:22-23

"But the God of all grace, who has called us unto His eternal glory by Christ Jesus, after that you have suffered a while, make you perfect, establish, strengthen, settle you." 1 Peter 5:10

"You have corrected others, and now I am correcting you. Submit to My pruning more of yourself. You will bear more of My fruit—kindness, mercy, compassion, joy, love, gentleness. All My children receive My correction. In everything, thank Me. Rejoice that I make amends and continually extend grace, and more grace."

October 26

"For it seemed good to the Holy Ghost, and to us, to lay upon you no greater burden than these necessary things."
Acts 15:28

"Blessed is every one that fears the Lord; that walks in His ways." *Psalm 128:1*

"Truly my soul waits upon God: from Him comes my salvation." *Psalm 62:1*

"You have made known to me the ways of life; You shall make me full of joy with Your countenance." *Acts 2:28*

"Give Me your burdens and concerns for others' lives. You can trust My ways when you don't know the future nor understand reasons for events or behavior. I have ways to reveal My will and My guidance that you know nothing of."

October 27

"The voice of the Lord came unto him, saying, I am the God of your fathers, the God of Abraham, and the God of Isaac, and the God of Jacob. Then Moses trembled and dare not behold." *Acts 7:31-32*

"We have found the Messiah, which is, being interpreted, the Christ."
John 1:41

"But I am poor and needy; yet the Lord thinks upon me: You are my help and my deliverer; make no tarrying, O my God." *Psalm 40:17*

"Blessed are they that keep His testimonies, and that seek Him with the whole heart." *Psalm 119:2*

"Yes, the people of Abraham, Isaac, and Jacob, through whom I have chosen to reveal Myself to all the world, will recognize Me as their own Messiah and deliverer. My Spirit is at work today among all whose hearts are seeking Me, the one, true, living God."

October 28

"I have also spoken by the prophets, and I have multiplied visions, and used similitudes, by the ministry of the prophets."
Hosea 12:10

"And he sought God in the days of Zechariah, who had understanding in the visions of God: and as long as he sought the Lord, God made him to prosper." *II Chronicles 26:5*

"As for these four children, God gave them knowledge and skill in all learning and wisdom: and Daniel had understanding in all visions and dreams." *Daniel 1:17*

"Happy is the man that finds wisdom, and the man that gets understanding." *Proverbs 3:13*

"Yes, My child, I often speak in pictures and symbols that the believing can interpret and understand. I show My prophetic revelations to those who will comprehend My message and use it wisely. I am clear and true and protective for those who will hear and see."

October 29

"Furthermore we have had fathers of our flesh which corrected us, and we gave them reverence: shall we not much rather be in subjection unto the Father of spirits and live?" Hebrews 12:9

Jesus said, "That you may be the children of your Father which is in Heaven: for He makes His sun to rise on the evil and on the good, and sends rain on the just and on the unjust." Matthew 5:45

Jesus said, "The harvest truly is plenteous, but the laborers are few." Matthew 9:37

Jesus said, "All power is given unto Me in Heaven and in earth." Matthew 28:18

"Am I not allowing correction to come to your character to bring forth more fruit? The rain must come to water and soften the seeds, not only in you, but in all the lives you touch. Many observe My work in you, and many draw from My Spirit in you. I always desire to extend My harvest. Rejoice that I use all things for My good because you, My child, are called to be an example of My power to transform a life and character."

October 30

"But unto everyone of us is given grace according to the measure of the gift of Christ. Wherefore He said, When He ascended up on high, He led captivity captive, and gave gifts unto men." Ephesians 4:7-8

You, "Being enriched in every thing to all bountifulness, which causes through us thanksgiving to God." II Corinthians 9:11

"When a man's ways please the Lord, He makes even his enemies to be at peace with him." Proverbs 16:7

"For we are the circumcision, which worship God in the Spirit, and rejoice in Christ Jesus, and have no confidence in the flesh." Philippians 3:3

"Everything good comes to you from My hand. I even turn the evil to good in some way. So, keep your heart thankful for even the small gifts and blessings. Place no faith in yourself, money, or possessions."

October 31

"And the Word was made flesh, and dwelt among us, (and we beheld His glory, the glory as of the only begotten of the Father,) full of grace and truth." John 1:14

"How then shall they call on Him in whom they have not believed? And how shall they believe in Him of whom they have not heard? And how shall they hear without a preacher?" Roman 10:14

"For He whom God has sent speaks the Words of God: for God gives not the Spirit by measure unto Him." John 3:34

"The blessing of the Lord, it makes rich, and He adds no sorrow with it." Proverbs 10:22

"Yes, I am the Word that speaks to all men, but they need a preacher; one to lead them directly. Be the one who speaks for Me; the one who supports others who speak for Me. Follow My leadings in peaceful generosity with all your resources."

November

November 1

"Enter into His gates with thanksgiving, and into His courts with praise: be thankful unto Him, and bless His Name."
Psalm 100:4

"Even them will I bring to My holy mountain, and make them joyful in My house of prayer."
Isaiah 56:7

Jesus said, "I am the good shepherd, and know My sheep, and am known of Mine."
John 10:14

Jesus said, "Feed My sheep." John 21:16

"Be one whose prayers are wrapped in joyful faith and thankful praise. Just to know Me, My heart, and My voice gives rise to faith and praise. You care for others because I care, and together our work answers prayer."

November 2

Jesus said of the devil, "When he speaks a lie, he speaks of his own: for he is a liar, and the father of it." John 8:44

"Why are you cast down, O my soul? And why are you disquieted in me? Hope you in God: for I shall yet praise Him for the help of His countenance." Psalm 42:5

Jesus said, "Woe unto the world because of offences! For it must needs be that offences come; but woe to that man by whom the offence comes!" Matthew 18:7

"Unto You, O my strength, will I sing: for God is my defense, and the God of my mercy." Psalm 59:17

"There will always be false reports, judgments, and criticism against My children. Learn what you must, but be not cast down or offended. I defend, vindicate, comfort, and restore My own, in My time, for a multitude of purposes."

November 3

"Wherefore gird up the loins of your mind, be sober, and hope to the end for the grace that is to be brought unto you at the revelation of Jesus Christ; as obedient children, not fashioning yourselves according to the former lusts in your ignorance."
1 Peter 1:13-14

Paul said, "I speak after the manner of men because of the infirmity of your flesh: for as you have yielded your members servants to uncleaness and to iniquity unto iniquity; even so now yield your members servants to righteousness unto holiness." Romans 6:19

"That I may know Him, and the power of His resurrection, and the fellowship of His sufferings, being made conformable unto His death." Philippians 3:10

"Surely the righteous shall give thanks unto Your Name: the upright shall dwell in Your presence." Psalm 140:13

"Obedience needs to be your prompt, loving response to Me. Trusting My Word and wisdom brings immediate yieldedness. Sharing in My sufferings when you are wronged deepens your fellowship with Me. Responding with My heart and mind makes My presence real."

November 4

"Call unto Me, and I will answer you, and show you great and mighty things, which you know not." Jeremiah 33:3

"I cried unto God with my voice, even unto God with my voice; and He gave ear unto me." Psalm 77:1

"But You, O Lord, are a shield for me; my glory, and the lifter up of my head." Psalm 3:3

"I will extol You, O Lord; for You have lifted me up, and have not made my foes to rejoice over me." Psalm 30:1

"Call upon Me in your times of trouble. I will bring the change in your attitude and responses to every day's challenges and events. Don't carry the troubles and be down-hearted. Lift them to Me, and I will lift your heart."

November 5

"Humble yourselves in the sight of the Lord, and He shall lift you up." James 4:10

"Charge them that are rich in this world, that they be not high minded, nor trust in uncertain riches, but in the living God, who gives us richly all things to enjoy." 1 Timothy 6:17

"Greater love has no man than this, that a man lay down his life for his friends." John 15:13

Jesus said, "For whosoever shall give you a cup of water to drink in My Name, because you belong to Christ, truly I say unto you, he shall not lose his reward." Mark 9:41

"Surrender, surrender, surrender all to Me—body, soul, and spirit. Lay aside your ideas of success and accomplishment. A little child is happy to be loved, to belong and to be valued. Know that you belong to me and are loved and valued. Extend this knowledge to those around you, living in the wonders I've created."

November 6

"Therefore I take pleasure in infirmities, in reproaches, in necessities, in persecutions, in distresses for Christ's sake: for when I am weak, then am I strong." II Corinthians 12:10

"And all that heard Him were astonished at His understanding and answers." Luke 2:47

"For what glory is it, if, when you be buffeted for your faults, you shall take it patiently? But if, when you do well, and suffer for it, you take it patiently, this is acceptable with God." 1 Peter 2:20

God, "Who has saved us, and called us with an holy calling, not according to our works, but according to His own purpose and grace, which was given us in Christ Jesus before the world began." II Timothy 1:9

"Dear One, when you recognize your weakness and quietly lay aside your solutions to life's dilemmas, you are ready to hear Mine and be used of Me in the places of need. Suffering is inevitable in every life. Embrace My purposes as I reveal them."

November 7

"This is a faithful saying, and worthy of all acceptation, that Christ Jesus came into the world to save sinners: of whom I am chief." 1 Timothy 1:15

"All the earth shall worship You, and sing unto You; they shall sing to Your Name. Selah." Psalm 66:4

Jesus said, "So the last shall be first, and the first last: for many be called, but few chosen." Matthew 20:16

"And that He died for all, that they which live should not henceforth live unto themselves, but unto Him which died for them, and rose again." II Corinthians 5:15

Moses, "Esteeming the reproach of Christ greater riches than the treasures in Egypt: for he had respect unto the recompense of the reward." Hebrews 11:26

"I came for all mankind, for all people and for all times. What could be more important than making Me known to all mankind? So, rejoice that you have been called and prepared to join in this work. Let it be known that you rejoice in My life and Words. All reproach and rejection falls on Me, not on you."

November 8

"You will keep him in perfect peace, whose mind is stayed on You: because he trusts in You." Isaiah 26:3

"For to be carnally minded is death; but to be spiritually minded is life and peace." Romans 8:6

"And above all things have fervent charity among yourselves: for charity shall cover the multitude of sins." 1 Peter 4:8

"Create in me a clean heart, O God; and renew a right spirit within me." Psalm 51:10

"When you are at peace with Me and at peace with yourself, you can appreciate all others as they are. Then you have no need or desire to seek for faults or project yours onto others. I say examine yourself to keep a clean temple, a clean heart, and a right spirit."

November 9

"Therefore we are buried with Him by baptism into death: that like as Christ was raised up from the dead by the glory of the Father, even so we also should walk in newness of life." Romans 6:4

"He must increase, but I must decrease." John 3:30

"For as many as are led by the Spirit of God, they are the sons of God." Romans 8:14

"Your Kingdom come. Your will be done in earth, as it is in Heaven." Matthew 6:10

"My dear child, resist not this new season. I lead ever onward into new places and thinking. It's always so more of Me and less of you can be manifested to others. I take you to new levels of Spirit controlled living on earth. This is how I answer your prayer for My will to be done on earth as it is in Heaven."

November 10

"But my God shall supply all your need according to His riches in glory by Christ Jesus." Philippians 4:19

"Pleasant words are as an honeycomb, sweet to the soul, and health to the bones." Proverbs 16:24

"And it shall come to pass in that day, that his burden shall be taken away from off your shoulder and his yoke from off your neck, and the yoke shall be destroyed because of the anointing." Isaiah 10:27

"To appoint unto them that mourn in Zion, to give unto them beauty for ashes, the oil of joy for mourning, the garment of praise for the spirit of heaviness; that they might be called trees of righteousness, the planting of the Lord, that He might be glorified." Isaiah 61:3

"My child, you see how sweetly and how easily you move under the power of My Spirit. You see how My love and joy and caring words flow through you. You see My yoke is easy and My burden is light. There's My oil of joy available to those who yield fully to My wise Spirit."

November 11

"I will instruct you and teach you in the way which you shall go: I will guide you with Mine eye." Psalm 32:8

"For with You is the fountain of life: in Your light shall we see light." Psalm 36:9

"Set your affections on things above, not on things on the earth." Colossians 3:2

"The Lord lifts up the meek: He casts the wicked down to the ground." Psalm 147:6

"I attend, guide, and speak into every detail of your life. You've invited Me in, and I am there. Much of what troubles and delays you is unimportant. Surrender your ideas and goals, and My peace and strength will lift you above the mundane."

November 12

"And you shall know that I am in the midst of Israel, and that I am the Lord your God, and none else: and My people shall never be ashamed." Joel 2:27

"Your Word is a lamp unto my feet, and a light unto my path." Psalm 119:105

Jesus said, "All things that the Father has are Mine: therefore said I, that He shall take of Mine, and shall show it unto you." John 16:15

"You therefore endure hardness, as a good soldier of Jesus Christ." II Timothy 2:3

"There is none besides Me. This simplifies your life. You can always reflect questions and problems to Me and My word. Listen and look for My voice and My light on your path. Truth is available when you seek Me with all your heart. Some truth will not be pleasant, but necessary for your growth and well being. Receive it all with gladness. I am the loving Father you need."

November 13

"I am as a wonder unto many; but You are my strong refuge." Psalm 71:7

"And you shall speak My words unto them, whether they will hear, or whether they will forbear: for they are most rebellious." Ezekiel 2:7

"And you shall hear of wars and rumours of wars: see that you be not troubled: for all these things must come to pass, but the end is not yet." Matthew 24:6

"But seek you first the Kingdom of God, and His righteousness; and all these things shall be added unto you." Matthew 6:33

"Yes, I am your refuge from the raging fires of gross sin, wars and rebellion. I still say not to fear. All is well with Me in My Kingdom. Continue to come to Me in all your need, and find My truth, wisdom and fellowship to be more than enough."

November 14

"My soul, wait you only upon God; for my expectation is from Him." Psalm 62:5

"Always in every prayer of mine for you all making request with joy, for your fellowship in the Gospel from the first day until now." Philippians 1:4

"Righteous are You, O Lord, and upright are Your judgments." Psalm 119:137

"But I trusted in You, O Lord: I said You are my God. My times are in Your hand." Psalm 31:14-15

"Wait upon Me in the many requests you have made for yourself and others. I agree with the intent and direction of your prayers, but the responses will be as I know best, in the time most fitting. Man often hinders what I would or could do for him. This is no reflection on your prayers."

November 15

Jesus said, "The first of all the commandments is, Hear, O Israel; the Lord our God is one Lord." Mark 12:29

Jesus said, "Greater love has no man than this, that a man lay down his life for his friends." John 15:13

Jesus said, "And this is life eternal, that they might know You the only true God, and Jesus Christ whom You have sent." John 17:3

"Looking unto Jesus the author and finisher of our faith; who for the joy that was set before Him endured the cross, despising the shame, and is set down at the right hand of the throne of God." Hebrews 12:2

"I am the One, the only true God and your Father, your source. I showed My great love for you on the cross. This is your clear message and commission."

November 16

Jesus said, "I can of mine own self do nothing: as I hear, I judge: and My judgment is just; because I seek not mine own will, but the will of the Father which has sent Me." John 5:30

"There is therefore now no condemnation to them which are in Christ Jesus, who walk not after the flesh, but after the Spirit." Romans 8:1

Jesus said, "And whosoever shall exalt himself shall be abased; and he that shall humble himself shall be exalted." Matthew 23:12

"Be not deceived; God is not mocked: for whatsoever a man sows, that shall he also reap." Galatians 6:7

"I am a just Father. I do not inflict guilt, shame and destruction. I allow you to see the consequences of your choices, if you are humble and willing to learn. I came to serve, save and satisfy your deepest needs. Recognize My law of sowing and reaping at work in you and in all My creation."

November 17

"For he put on righteousness as a breastplate, and an helmet of salvation upon his head." Isaiah 59:17

*"And you fathers, provoke not your children to wrath: but bring them up in the
nurture and admonition of the Lord."* Ephesians 6:4

Jesus said, "the Kingdom of God is within you." Luke 17:21

Jesus said, "And what I say unto you I say unto all, Watch." Mark 13:37

"Put on the breastplate of righteousness, and listen to every small word of admonition from
Me. Look within to My Kingdom for your worth and purpose, knowing My joy in every
circumstance. Watch and wait on Me in peace."

November 18

*"Neither is there salvation in any other: for there is none other Name under heaven given among
men, whereby we must be saved."* Acts 4:12

*Jesus said, "I am the vine, you are the branches: He that abides in Me, and I in him, the same brings
forth much fruit: for without Me you can do nothing."* John 15:5

*Jesus said, "It is the Spirit that quickens; the flesh profits nothing: the words that I speak unto you, they are Spirit and
they are life."* John 6:63

"For we are laborers together with God: you are God's husbandry, you are God's building." 1 Corinthians 3:9

"You can save no one. You cannot effect the changes you would like in others. Even in yourself, you
need Me to give the inner life and truth you need in order to be transformed into the likeness of Me,
your Creator. Find peace in this. Come to Me with your requests. Together we will effect changes and
transformations."

November 19

Jesus said, "Truly, truly, I say unto you, He that hears My Word, and believes on Him that sent Me, has everlasting life, and shall not come into condemnation; but is passed from death into life." John 5:24

"For in Him we live, and move, and have our being." Acts 17:28

"For You are my hope, O Lord God: You are my trust from my youth." Psalm 71:5

"And whatsoever you do, do it heartily, as to the Lord, and not unto men; Knowing that of the Lord you shall receive the reward of the inheritance: for you serve the Lord Jesus Christ." Colossians 3:23-24

"Yes, I am your life. In Me, you live and breathe and have your being. In Me is well being, and ever springing hope. Receive of My abundance, for it's your inheritance now."

November 20

"O continue Your loving kindness unto them that know you; and Your righteousness to the upright in heart." Psalm 36:10

Jesus said, "What I do you know not now; but you shall know hereafter." John 13:7

"And they shall see His face; and His Name shall be in their foreheads." Revelation 22:4

"But Jesus answered them, My Father works hitherto, and I work." John 5:17

"You know enough of Me, My child, to keep you knowing more and more. The complete picture will come when we meet face to face. Much of what concerns you now on earth is not to be your concern. Contrary to appearances, I am greatly at work, and always in control."

November 21

"Let your light so shine before men, that they may see your good works, and glorify your Father which is in heaven."
Matthew 5:16

"That you may be blameless and harmless, the sons of God, without rebuke, in the midst of a crooked and perverse nation, among whom you shine as lights in the world." Philippians 2:15

"Hereby know we that we dwell in Him, and He in us, because He has given us of His spirit." 1 John 4:13

"For we know that the whole creation groans and travails in pain together until now." Romans 8:22

"I would have you to shine in the best and worst of life on earth. My Spirit in you knows how to rightly respond in all situations and relationships. Let Him lead and show you. This removes the burdens and eases the pain."

November 22

"But we speak the wisdom of God in a mystery, even the hidden wisdom, which God ordained before the world unto our glory." 1 Corinthians 2:7

"Wherein He has abounded toward us in all wisdom and prudence; Having made known unto us the mystery of His will, according to His good pleasure which He has purposed in Himself." Ephesians 1:8-9

"Fight the good fight of faith, lay hold on eternal life, whereunto you are also called, and have professed a good profession among many witnesses." 1 Timothy 6:12

"And this Gospel of the Kingdom shall be preached in all the world for a witness unto all nations; and then shall the end come." Matthew 24:14

"My ways are often hidden, and so far above your understanding. This must be, for My good plans are vast and lead to My ongoing, unknowable purposes. Your life is a minute piece of an earthly story. Be faithful to hold fast to My truth when you do not understand. My Kingdom is where you must live in righteousness, peace, and joy in My Holy Spirit. This is enough."

November 23

"Now concerning spiritual gifts, brethren, I would not have you ignorant." 1 Corinthians 12:1

"Now there are diversities of gifts, but the same Spirit." 1 Corinthians 12:4

"But he that prophesies speaks unto men to edification, and exhortation, and comfort." 1 Corinthians 14:3

"Follow after charity, and desire spiritual gifts, but rather that you may prophesy." 1 Corinthians 14:1

"I have given you the gift to see beyond the appearances and discern the spiritual reality. This gift is for My purposes, to encourage, comfort, and build up My people; to give evidence of My all knowing Spirit of truth and love. Let your motivation be as Mine is."

November 24

"There remains therefore a rest to the people of God." Hebrews 4:9

"What man is he that fears the Lord? Him shall He teach in the way that He shall choose. His soul shall dwell at ease; and his seed shall inherit the earth." Psalm 25:12-13

"And they were all amazed, and were in doubt, saying one to another, What means this? Others mocking said, These men are full of new wine." Acts 2:12-13

Jesus said, "John indeed baptized with water; but you shall be baptized with the Holy Ghost." Acts 11:16

"Take My rest. Take My peace. Find how easy it is to follow My Spirit. Your inner life should direct and fulfill your outer life. Do not expect all to understand a life in the Holy Spirit."

November 25

"In every thing give thanks: for this is the will of God in Christ Jesus concerning you." 1 Thessalonians 5:18

Jesus said, "Blessed are the peacemakers: for they shall be called the children of God." Matthew 5:9

"That at the Name of Jesus every knee should bow, of things in heaven, and things in earth, and things under the earth." Philippians 2:10

"Glory to God in the highest, and on earth peace, good will toward men." Luke 2:14

"The time to be thankful is every time and at all times. The peace I offer cannot be found anywhere else. Even the paths that lead downward must all eventually end before Me, your Creator. My heart's desire is for all to come to know Me and My endless love."

November 26

Jesus said, "It is more blessed to give than to receive." Acts 20:35

Jesus said, "Blessed are the merciful: for they shall obtain mercy." Matthew 5:7

Jesus said, "He that has ears to hear, let him hear." Matthew 11:15

Jesus said, "If any man serve Me, let him follow Me; and where I am, there shall also My servant be: if any man serve Me, him will My Father honor." John 12:26

"Give and give as I give, freely and compassionately. Have no concern for your future needs. See and hear with your spirit as I speak. Follow My lead continuously, concentrating on today's moments. I hold and carry the future."

November 27

Jesus said, "If you shall ask anything in My Name, I will do it." John 14:14

Jesus said, "For with God, nothing shall be impossible." Luke 1:37

Jesus said, "But go rather to the lost sheep of the house of Israel." Matthew 10:6

Jesus said, "He that finds his life shall lose it: and he that loses his life for My sake shall find it." Matthew 10:39

"Ask and seek My highest for yourself and others. See yourself and others as they could be in My will. Join your vision to Mine of what could be. No person or situation is without hope if yielded to Me. This is the great labor to which you and My disciples are called. Go and make disciples, baptizing them in My Name. This is life at its most glorious."

November 28

"Not that I speak in respect of want: for I have learned, in whatsoever state I am, therewith to be content."
Philippians 4:11

Jesus said, "And before Him shall be gathered all nations; and He shall separate them one from another, as a shepherd divides his sheep from the goats." Matthew 25:32

"Multitudes, multitudes in the valley of decision: for the day of the Lord is near in the valley of decision." Joel 3:14

"All the ends of the world shall remember and turn unto the Lord: and all the kindreds of the nations shall worship before You." Psalm 22:27

"Be content. Yes, keep a grateful heart always. I've called you to a labor of prayer for your nation and other nations. Maintain My heart for them. This day, many are considering and examining their life's worth and peace. Continue asking for a wave of turning to Me and My will and My righteousness."

November 29

"Believe you not that I am in the Father, and the Father in Me? The Words that I speak unto you I speak not of Myself: but the Father that dwells in Me, He does the works." John 14:10

"The heavens declare the glory of God; and the firmament shows His handiwork." Psalm 19:1

"Blessed are the pure in heart: for they shall see God." Matthew 5:8

"But You are holy, O You that inhabits the praises of Israel." Psalm 22:3

"I am always speaking in some way. It is I speaking when your earth revolves and you observe the heavens. It is the needy in spirit who take notice of Me and decide to listen, see and experience Me. I enjoy that My children respond to Me."

November 30

"In God is my salvation and my glory: the rock of my strength, and my refuge, is in God." Psalm 62:7

"I have set the Lord always before me: because He is at my right hand, I shall not be moved. Therefore my heart is glad, and my glory rejoices: my flesh also shall rest in hope." Psalm 16:8-9

"Grace be unto you, and peace, from God our Father, and from the Lord Jesus Christ." 1 Corinthians 1:3

"Yet I will rejoice in the Lord, I will joy in the God of my salvation." Habakkuk 3:18

"Yes, I am your safe haven, always present, always protecting, as you call on Me. Few of mankind truly understand this, and retreat to Me continually. When I say, "Come unto Me," I say this because you cannot find rest or peace or joy anywhere else. I know your need."

December

December 1

"... a time to keep silence, and a time to speak ...." *Ecclesiastes 3:7*

"And the Spirit and the Bride say, Come. And let him that hears say, Come. And let him that is thirsty come.
And whosoever will, let him take the water of life freely." *Revelation 22:17*

"And suddenly there came a sound from Heaven as of a rushing mighty wind, and it filled all the house where they were sitting." *Acts 2:2*

"And to make all men see what is the fellowship of the mystery, which from the beginning of the world has been hid in God, who created all things by Jesus Christ." *Ephesians 3:9*

"Mankind often longs to draw away from the world of noise to the quiet of natural surroundings. In this, they long for Me; for the flowing, living waters and refreshing breezes of My Spirit. All My creation around you speaks of Me. I alone am the source of every need and your life's purpose."

December 2

"Behold, to obey is better than sacrifice." 1 Samuel 15:22

Jesus said, "It is written, That man shall not live by bread alone, but by every Word of God." Luke 4:4

"You see then how that by works a man is justified, and not by faith only." James 2:24

"Whoso boasts himself of a false gift is like clouds and wind without rain." Proverbs 25:14

"Effectual prayer and immediate obedience to My Words will bring the ongoing flow of life you desire. Your faith in Me must be followed by action and works. The clouds must bring rain and even times of cooling shade."

December 3

"I have made the earth, and created man upon it: I, even My hands, have stretched out the heavens, and all their host have I commanded." Isaiah 45:12

"The Lord God, merciful and gracious, long suffering, and abundant in goodness and truth." Exodus 34:6

"Stand fast therefore in the liberty wherewith Christ has made us free, and be not entangled again with the yoke of bondage." Galatians 5:1

"And you became followers of us, and of the Lord, having received the Word in much affliction, with joy of the Holy Ghost." 1 Thessalonians 1:6

"I provide all things in the sun, the wind, the earth and the stars. Avail yourself of My abundant gifts. Find healing and joy in the free flowing winds with Me. I am the great giver. Be a great receiver."

December 4

"The liberal soul shall be made fat: and he that waters shall be watered also himself." Proverbs 11:25

Jesus said, "If you will be perfect, go and sell that you have, and give to the poor, and you shall have treasure in Heaven: and come and follow Me." Matthew 19:21

Jesus said, "But love you your enemies, and do good, and lend, hoping for nothing again; and your reward shall be great, and you shall be the children of the Highest: for He is kind unto the unthankful and to the evil." Luke 6:35

Jesus said, "But when you do alms, let not your left hand know what your right hand does: That your alms may be in secret: and your Father which sees in secret Himself shall reward you openly." Matthew 6:3-4

"Imitate Me by giving. Give, give, give and live the full rich life I desire for you. Always be looking for My ways to give. Give your time, your talents, your treasure where I direct, with no thought of return. I see and know it all, and I reward accordingly in some way, at some time. Have no thought for man's approval or praise. Quietly serve in My Kingdom."

December 5

Jesus said, "After this manner therefore pray you: Our Father which art in Heaven, Hallowed be Your Name. Your Kingdom come. Your will be done in earth, as it is in Heaven." Matthew 6:9-10

"The fear of the Lord is the beginning of wisdom: a good understanding have all they that do His commandments: His praise endures forever." Psalm 111:10

"The secret of the Lord is with them that fear Him; and He will show them His covenant." Psalm 25:14

"The Lord will perfect that which concerns me: Your mercy, O Lord, endures forever: forsake not the works of Your own hands." Psalm 138:8

"Pray continually. Let all that comes before you be the subject of conversation with Me. Fearful reverence for My will and Words in all matters brings wisdom and right responses to all circumstances."

December 6

"For this is good and acceptable in the sight of God our Saviour; Who will have all men to be saved, and to come unto the knowledge of the truth." 1 Timothy 2:3-4

Jesus said, "For God sent not His Son into the world to condemn the world; but that the world through Him might be saved." John 3:17

"I will go in the strength of the Lord God: I will make mention of Your righteousness, even of Yours only." Psalm 71:16

"For the promise is unto you, and to your children, and to all that are afar off, even as many as the Lord our God shall call." Acts 2:39

"Dear Ones, remember My Words to you—go and make disciples. I bring ones to you from afar. Welcome them and tell them about Me. I would that all would hear and be saved."

December 7

Jesus said, "And you shall be hated of all men for My Name's sake." Luke 21:17

"Arise, shine: for your light is come, and the glory of the Lord is risen upon you." Isaiah 60:1

"...for the Lord sees not as man sees; for man looks on the outward appearance, but the Lord looks on the heart."
1 Samuel 16:7

"And even to your old age I am He; and even to hoar hairs will I carry you: I have made, and I will bear;
even I will carry, and will deliver you." Isaiah 46:4

"Do not trouble yourself with the opinions and responses of others. Shine forth My loving care and honor for others. This is the purpose, the mission I have called you to. Remember, I see the heart. Appearance can be deceptive. Aging is a season of richness, revelation, and gracious acceptance. Rejoice in every season, My child."

December 8

Jesus said, "The time is fulfilled, and the Kingdom of God is at hand: repent you, and believe the Gospel." Mark 1:15

Jesus said, "Fear not, little flock; for it is your Father's good pleasure to give you the Kingdom." Luke 12:32

Jesus said, "Truly I say unto you, There is no man that has left house, or parents, or brethren, or wife, or children, for the Kingdom of God's sake, Who shall not receive manifold more in this present time, and in the world to come
life everlasting." Luke 18:29-30

Jesus said, "Truly, truly, I say unto you, Except a man be born again, he cannot see the Kingdom of God." John 3:3

"My Kingdom has come and My Kingdom is eternal. It's your limited understanding of My Kingdom that gives you conflict on earth. But, for those who enter My Kingdom as My children, all the glory and riches are available in eternal measure."

December 9

"A merry heart does good like a medicine: but a broken spirit dries the bones." Proverbs 17:22

"…he that is of a merry heart has a continual feast." Proverbs 15:15

"…he that is of God hears God's Words." John 8:47

"I will give unto him that is thirsty of the fountain of the water of life freely." Revelation 21:6

"There is a time for laughter and making merry among yourselves. But, remember Me, and pray for My Spirit to guide your thoughts and conversations. Value, above all, the quiet time we spend together. Be rejuvenated in the silent listening to Me, basking in My presence. There, you are enriched to overflow among others."

December 10

"Speak, Lord; for your servant hears." 1 Samuel 3:9

"I will hear what God the Lord will speak: for He will speak peace unto His people, and to His saints: but let them not turn again to folly." Psalm 85:8

Jesus said, "Henceforth I call you not servants; for the servant knows not what his Lord does: but I have called you friends, for all things that I have heard of My Father I have made known unto you." John 15:15

"My son, attend unto My wisdom, and bow your ear to My understanding: that you may regard discretion, and that your lips may keep knowledge." Proverbs 5:1-2

"Be assured that I am always speaking, always available to My children. You can train your ears to My voice by enjoying My closeness, friendship, and love. We can understand one another and use no words."

December 11

"*Remember His marvelous works that He has done; His wonders, and the judgments of His mouth.*" Psalm 105:5

"*Let the words of my mouth, and the meditation of my heart, be acceptable in your sight, O Lord, my strength, and my redeemer.*" Psalm 19:14

"*…for your Father knows what things you have need of, before you ask Him.*" Matthew 6:8

"*And I sought for a man among them, that should make up the hedge, and stand in the gap before Me for the land, that I should not destroy it: but I found none.*" Ezekiel 22:30

"My Spirit brings to your thoughts what I would have you remember, meditate on, and draw wisdom from. I also remind you of the needs of others far off and close. Therefore, you are able to act somehow on their behalf, standing often for them."

December 12

"Let all those that seek You rejoice and be glad in You: and let such as love Your salvation say continually, Let God be magnified." Psalm 70:4

"But let him that glories glory in this, that he understands and knows Me, that I am the Lord which exercise lovingkindness, judgment, and righteousness, in the earth: for in these things I rejoice, says the Lord." Jeremiah 9:24

"That you might walk worthy of the Lord unto all pleasing, being fruitful in every good work, and increasing the knowledge of God; Strengthened with all might, according to His glorious power, unto all patience and longsuffering with joyfulness." Colossians 1:10-11

"Blessing, and glory, and wisdom, and thanksgiving, and honour, and power, and might, be unto our God forever and ever. Amen." Revelation 7:12

"Rejoicing is the only response appropriate to my poured out love. When your eyes and ears are opened to My Spirit working and radiating all around you, the wonders and glory lift your heart to Me in rejoicing thanksgiving."

December 13

"And Jesus went about all the cities and villages, teaching in their synagogues, and preaching the Gospel of the Kingdom, and healing every sickness and every disease among the people." Matthew 9:35

"...to another the gifts of healing by the same Spirit." 1 Corinthians 12:9

"For the gifts and calling of God are without repentance." Romans 11:29

"Beloved, I wish above all things that you may prosper and be in health, even as your soul prospers." III John 2

"It is My life power that radiates healing to all that is damaged. There are gifts of healing available to those who choose to help in My healing power. My gifts and callings are without regrets. There is satisfaction, joy, and reward for those who receive a heart to heal."

December 14

How precious also are your thoughts unto me, O God, how great is the sum of them!" Psalm 139:17

"O Lord, how great are your works! And your thoughts are very deep." Psalm 92:5

"And God said, 'Let us make man in our image, after our likeness.'" Genesis 1:26

"But grow in grace, and in the knowledge of our Lord and Saviour Jesus Christ. To Him be glory both now and forever. Amen." II Peter 3:18

"All My thoughts toward you are incomprehensible to you now. They are always new and always good. Truly, you are created in My image for My pleasure. I am your true Father, your Creator. Can you not understand that I enjoy our companionship and seeing you grow?"

December 15

"The Lord preserves the strangers; He relieves the fatherless and widows." Psalm 146:9

Jesus said, "For I was hungry, and you gave Me meat: I was thirsty, and you gave Me drink: I was a stranger and you took Me in." Matthew 25:35

"Be not forgetful to entertain strangers: for thereby some have entertained angels unawares." Hebrews 13:2

"Use hospitality one to another without grudging." 1 Peter 4:9

"Bless and care for the stranger among you. You will entertain angels unknowingly. I send many to you who need tender care such as I give. Let them see and hear that your God lives and hears prayer. My children, practice hospitality."

December 16

"Wherefore seeing we also are compassed about with so great a cloud of witnesses, let us lay aside every weight, and the sin which does so easily beset us, and let us run with patience the race that is set before us." Hebrews 12:1

"The Lord knows how to deliver the Godly out of temptations, and to reserve the unjust unto the day of judgment to be punished." II Peter 2:9

Jesus said, "By this shall all men know that you are My disciples, if you have love one to another." John 13:35

"For whatsoever is born of God overcomes the world: and this is the victory that overcomes the world, even our faith." 1 John 5:4

"Set your mind on the goal before you. Many are the common temptations and distractions. A disciple must discipline and train themself to continually remain on the narrow path that leads to life, now and into eternity. This path becomes narrower in interest as you leave the world's goals behind. Fear not this concentration and surrender."

December 17

Jesus said, "For even the Son of man came not to be ministered unto, but to minister, and to give His life a ransom for many." Matthew 20:28

Jesus said, "You call Me Master and Lord: and you say well; for so I am." John 13:13

"And I intreat you also, true yokefellow." Philippians 4:3

Jesus said, "Take My yoke upon you, and learn of Me; for I am meek and lowly in heart: and you shall find rest unto your souls. For My yoke is easy, and My burden is light." Matthew 11:29-30

"I am not a taskmaster. I am Master of all. Recognize your value, dignity, and place in My Kingdom's order. This adds to your peace, contentment, and blessing. I ask you to only share My yoke; that which you can do easily. I will remove the heaviness."

December 18

"He has made everything beautiful in His time." Ecclesiastes 3:11

"...the goodness of God leads you to repentance." Romans 2:4

"But if we walk in the light, as He is in the light, we have fellowship one with another, and the blood of Jesus Christ His Son cleanses us from all sin." 1 John 1:7

"Humble yourselves therefore under the mighty hand of God, that He may exalt you in due time." 1 Peter 5:6

"Resist not My efforts to beautify you. Confession, true repentance, forgiveness, obedience all make you clean within and bring the beauty of holiness. So humble yourself under My hand of workmanship. Desire My true beauty."

December 19

Jesus said, "Watch and pray, that you enter not into temptation: the spirit indeed is willing, but the flesh is weak."
Matthew 26:41

"Therefore I take pleasure in infirmities, in reproaches, in necessities, in persecutions, in distresses for Christ's sake: for when I am weak, then am I strong." II Corinthians 12:10

Jesus said, "You shall love the Lord your God with all your heart, and with all your soul, and with all your mind."
Matthew 22:37

Jesus said, "And seek not you what you shall eat, or what you shall drink, neither be you of doubtful mind. For all these things do the nations of the world seek after: and your Father knows that you have need of these things." Luke 12:29-30

"My child, all have areas of human weakness. Recognize and confess your need for My strength where you are weak. Your love for Me and My Father will grow rich and strong as you acknowledge your needs and receive My supply."

December 20

Jesus said, "And when you shall hear of wars and rumors of wars, be you not troubled: for such things must needs be; but the end shall not be yet." Mark 13:7

Jesus said, "For in those days shall be affliction, such as was not from the beginning of the creation which God created unto this time, neither shall be." Mark 13:19

Jesus said, "And then shall they see the Son of Man coming in the clouds with great power and glory." Mark 13:26

Jesus said, "Heaven and earth shall pass away: but My Words shall not pass away." Mark 13:31

"Be not discouraged by the great trouble and pain that has come upon the earth again. Have I not said that these disasters and depravities must come before My return? Look up. Prepare yourself to see Me. Surely, I keep My Word."

December 21

"For all the promises of God in Him are yea, and in Him Amen, unto the glory of God by us." II Corinthians 1:20

Jesus said, "But let your communication be, Yea, yea; Nay, nay: for whatsoever is more than these comes of evil." Matthew 5:37

"And the angel said unto them, Fear not: for, behold, I bring you good tidings of great joy, which shall be to all people." Luke 2:10

"There is no fear in love; but perfect love casts out fear: because fear has torment. He that fears is not made perfect in love." 1 John 4:18

"All My ways are yes and amen. They leave no room for fear."

December 22

Jesus said, "Consider the lilies of the field, how they grow; they toil not, neither do they spin." Matthew 6:28

"the heavens are the work of Your hands." Psalm 102:25

"...there is a Friend that sticks closer than a brother." Proverbs 18:24

"...you rejoice with joy unspeakable and full of glory." 1 Peter 1:8

"Consider the stars. Consider the lilies. Consider the minute workings of My handiwork in you and in all you perceive. Let jubilation arise in your heart, close to My heart. Truly, it is joy beyond words, and full of radiant glory."

December 23

Jesus said, "And the cares of this world, and the deceitfulness of riches, and the lusts of other things entering in, choke the Word, and it becomes unfruitful." Mark 4:19

"I bare you on eagles' wings, and brought you unto Myself." Exodus 19:4

"And He has raised us up together, and made us sit together in Heavenly places in Christ Jesus." Ephesians 2:6

"Be sober, be vigilant; because your adversary the devil, as a roaring lion, walks about, seeking whom he may devour: whom resist steadfast in the faith, knowing that the same afflictions are accomplished in your brethren that are in the world." 1 Peter 5:8-9

"The pressures of this world and selfishness will always attempt to encroach on your righteousness, peace and joy. Take the eagle perspective of waiting, while sitting with me in Heavenly places. Rise above, wait on Me, and resist evil in My Name."

December 24

He that has My commandments, and keeps them, he it is that loves Me: and he that loves Me shall be loved of My Father, and I will love him, and will manifest myself to him. John 14:21

Jesus prayed, "And now come I to You; and these things I speak in the world, that they might have My joy fulfilled in themselves." John 17:13

"But know that the Lord has set apart him that is Godly for Himself." Psalm 4:3

"The gift of God is eternal life through Jesus Christ our Lord." Romans 6:23

"How rich, how beyond wonder is your life with Me. You grow by My revelation of Myself to you alone. This is how you move from glory to glory in sanctification. (See II Cor. 3:18.) I have called you. I have set you apart in your world, and I desire you to most enjoy the gift of My Son and all the eternal gifts He brings you."

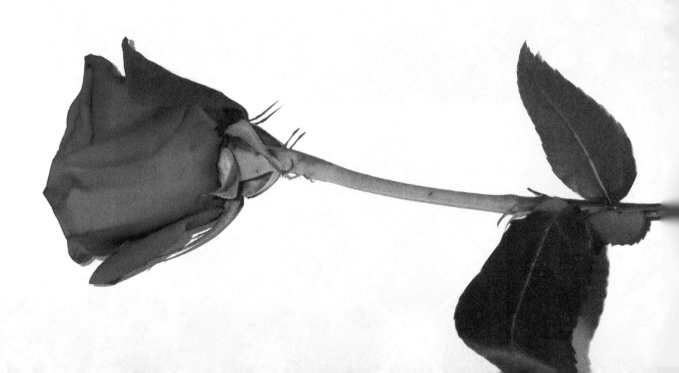

December 25

"For unto us a child is born, unto us a Son is given: and the government shall be upon His shoulder: and His Name shall be called Wonderful, Counsellor, The Mighty God, The Everlasting Father, The Prince of Peace." Isaiah 9:6

"And she brought forth her firstborn Son, and wrapped Him in swaddling clothes, and laid Him in a manger; because there was no room for them in the inn." Luke 2:7

"For unto you is born this day in the city of David a Saviour, which is Christ the Lord. ... Glory to God in the highest, and on earth peace, good will toward men." Luke 2:11, 14

Jesus said. "Ask, and it shall be given you; seek, and you shall find: knock, and it shall be opened unto you." Matthew 7:7

"My peace I give to you. How precious My peace is in your world where many are ever searching for consolation, worth, and security. I am the great giver, and it is My joy when you receive well My peace."

December 26

"As you know how we exhorted and comforted and charged every one of you, as a father does his children, that you would walk worthy of God, who has called you unto His Kingdom and glory." 1 Thessalonians 2:11-12

Jesus said, "If you knew the gift of God, and who it is that says to you, Give Me to drink; you would have asked of Him, and He would have given you Living water." John 4:10

"Be not overcome of evil, but overcome evil with good." Romans 12:21

"In this was manifested the love of God toward us, because that God sent His only begotten Son into the world, that we might live through Him." 1 John 4:9

"Fear not, little Ones, it is My joy to give you the Kingdom. (See Luke 12:32.) My Kingdom is an ever springing up of Living waters, meeting every need and overcoming. It overcomes all that self is prey to and tempted by. Haven't I given you My best, My only Son to show My great love for you, and made available every abundant provision of My Kingdom?"

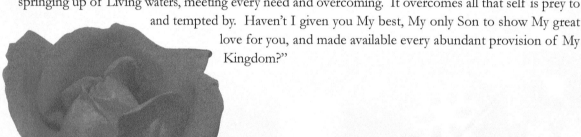

December 27

"Whoso keeps the law is a wise son: but he that is a companion of riotous men shames his father." Proverbs 28:7

Jesus said, "For I have given you an example, that you should do as I have done to you." John 13:15

"But continue you in the things which you have learned and have been assured of, knowing of whom you have learned them; And that from a child you have known the holy Scriptures, which are able to make you wise unto salvation through faith which is in Christ Jesus." II Timothy 3:14-15

"All Scripture is given by inspiration of God, and is profitable for doctrine, for reproof, for correction, for instruction in righteousness: that the man of God may be perfect, thoroughly furnished unto all good works." II Timothy 3:16-17

"Allow Me to choose your closest relationships. There is much to be learned from others. I create a circle of examples and influences around you that you may learn My ways, discernment, and wisdom. Your first, close fellowship with Me establishes what you will learn from others."

December 28

"Being confident of this very thing, that He which has begun a good work in you will perform it until the day of Jesus Christ." Philippians 1:6

"For now we see through a glass, darkly; but then face to face: now I know in part; but then shall I know even as also I am known." 1 Corinthians 13:12

"Having therefore, brethren, boldness to enter into the holiest by the blood of Jesus, by a new and living way, which He has consecrated for us through the veil, that is to say, His flesh." Hebrews 10:19-20

"Cast not away therefore your confidence, which has great recompence of reward." Hebrews 10:35

"Be confident that what I say to you is true. Remember, you see through the veil and only in part. I know the whole. Your part is to trust Me, what I say, and who I am. Those who believe enjoy riches the unbeliever cannot imagine."

December 29

"Praise Him, you heavens of heavens, and you waters that be above the heavens. Let them praise the Name of the Lord: for He commanded, and they were created." Psalm 148:4-5

"Now unto the King eternal, immortal, invisible, the only wise God, be honor and glory forever and ever. Amen." 1 Timothy 1:17

"Now the God of peace, that brought again from the dead our Lord Jesus, that great shepherd of the sheep, through the blood of the everlasting covenant, make you perfect in every good work to do His will, working in you that which is well pleasing in His sight, through Jesus Christ; to whom be glory forever and ever. Amen." Hebrews 13:20-21

"Yes, though I walk through the valley of the shadow of death, I will fear no evil: for You are with me; Your rod and Your staff they comfort me." Psalm 23:4

"The unseen world is where My work and transformation begin. My Word creates. Man tries to alter My truth and work, opening himself to destructive forces, but My Word and My work continue without interruption. Agree with Me and align yourself with My Word and work, and do not fear the evil one."

December 30

"And another angel came out of the temple, crying with a loud voice to Him that sat on the cloud, thrust in your sickle, and reap: for the time is come for you to reap; for the harvest of the earth is ripe." Revelation 14:15

"That in the ages to come He might show the exceeding riches of His grace in His kindness toward us through Christ Jesus." Ephesians 2:7

"Who by the mouth of Your servant David has said, Why did the heathen rage, and the people imagine vain things?" Acts 4:25

"And your ears shall hear a Word behind you, saying, This is the way, walk you in it, when you turn to the right hand, and when you turn to the left." Isaiah 30:21

"All time and all things are in My hands. My plan is unfolding through earth's ages. O, that man would desire to know Me through My Son. My outcome will not be thwarted, though the nations rage and go astray. Be about My humble work, showing the way, the truth, and the life. Attune your ears to Me for the wise counsel you need always."

December 31

"As for Me, this is My covenant with them, says the Lord; My Spirit that is upon you, and My Words which I have put in your mouth, shall not depart out of your mouth, … says the Lord, from henceforth and forever." Isaiah 59:21

"But let us, who are of the day, be sober, putting on the breast plate of faith and love; and for an helmet, the hope of salvation. For God has not appointed us to wrath, but to obtain salvation by our Lord Jesus Christ."
1 Thessalonians 5:8-9

"Shew me Your ways, O Lord; teach me Your paths. Lead me in Your truth, and teach me: for You are the God of my salvation; on You do I wait all the day." Psalm 25:4-5

"But thanks be to God, which gives us the victory through our Lord Jesus Christ." 1 Corinthians 15:57

"I will sing of the mercies of the Lord forever: with my mouth I will make known Your faithfulness to all generations."
Psalm 89:1

"As your year in time closes, remember, Mine never closes. My arms and My Kingdom of loving justice are ever open to whosoever will come. Look ahead with Me and know that My ways are bringing you to greater victory and knowledge of Me—all Truth."

Rose Petals

is available at:

oliepresspublisher.com

amazon.com

barnesandnoble.com

christianbook.com

deepershopping.com

and other online stores

Store managers:

Order wholesale through:

Ingram Book Company or

Spring Arbor

or by emailing:

olivepressbooks@gmail.com

CPSIA information can be obtained
at www.ICGtesting.com
Printed in the USA
BVHW02s2137081018
529649BV00004B/18/P